19TH CENTURY BASEBALL IN CHICAGO

WOODCUT OF HALL OF FAMER CAPTAIN ADRIAN "CAP" ANSON. Anson played for the Chicago White Stockings from 1876 to 1897, hitting over .300 in all but two of those years. He became the first player in major league history to collect 3000 hits. (Photo Courtesy of Transcendental Graphics.)

19TH CENTURY BASEBALL IN CHICAGO

Mark Rucker and John Freyer

ARCADIA

Copyright © 2003 by Mark Rucker and John Freyer.
ISBN 0-7385-3181-2

Published by Arcadia Publishing,
an imprint of Tempus Publishing, Inc.
2 Cumberland Street
Charleston, SC 29401

Printed in Great Britain.

Library of Congress Catalog Card Number: Applied For.

For all general information contact Arcadia Publishing at:
Telephone 843-853-2070
Fax 843-853-0044
E-Mail sales@arcadiapublishing.com

For customer service and orders:
Toll-Free 1-888-313-2665

Visit us on the internet at http://www.arcadiapublishing.com

CONTENTS

ACKNOWLEDGMENTS

There are many people that played a part in the eventual publishing of my first book. This is a compilation of years of research. My fascination about the birth of the game led me down several paths: playing vintage baseball, researching 1800s baseball and collecting as many images of the sport that I could find.

The following people played the largest role and I want to sincerely thank each and every one:

To my wife, Carrie, whose patience is unparalleled. She never tires of listening to my discoveries. She has quietly pushed me forward.

My son, Jack, helped me with some illustrations and his honest opinion is unfaltering. Since he came to the earth, he has opened my eyes to a new world of wonderment.

Mark Rucker, who has become a wonderful friend and who has the most brilliant eye for the true beauty in images.

Ted Hathaway, a topnotch researcher, who helped me unlock the past in print. I couldn't have finished this without Ted.

John Husman and Frederick Ivor-Campbell, whose initial kindness has sent me on a journey that will never end.

Allison Barash and Priscilla Astifan, whose friendship I cherish and who fed my mind with wonderful thoughts of baseball.

Marilyn Seaman, the cheapest typist and the most wonderful mother-in-law a guy could ever hope to have.

Dean Thilgen, whose tireless search for knowledge never ceases to amaze me.

Mark Heppner and Doc Lawson, who got me hooked on the vintage base ball bug. I will always consider them friends.

Coot Hunkele, the most unselfish researcher I've met. He asks the most intelligent questions and stirs my thoughts.

Lefty Trudeau and Ken and Paula Weaver, whose frankness, honesty, and pursuit of true vintage reproductions are truly appreciated.

Joanna Shearer and the Deep River Grinders, whose love for the game of "Base Ball" taught me many lessons about teamwork, pride and clockwork defense. Hip, Hip, Huzzah!

Society for the American Base Ball Research (SABR) 19th Century Committee for posting tidbits of information that makes reading e-mails worthwhile.

The Vintage Base Ball Association (VBBA) for letting me get involved as publisher for all these years.

Fellow Quigley alum Marty Cusack, of the Chicago Historical Society, who can answer questions that I have no answer for.

Jeff Ruetsche of Arcadia Publishing, who walked me through the whole process, quietly prodding me along. He has become a good friend and ally.

My dad, Jack "Stinky" Freyer, who has endured every goofy idea I ever had.

And lastly, to my mother, Mary Jane, who passed away in October 2002. She, like she always was, would have been very proud of me.

INTRODUCTION

The birth of baseball is a term that contradicts itself. Baseball was not born. It was not invented. It has evolved. Or, in the words of heralded 19th-Century statistician and baseball analyst, Henry Chadwick, "Base ball wasn't invented, it jes' growed."

The mention of ball games in America dates back to as early as 1775. In recent years, thanks to the advance of technology in research, passages have been found that make reference to a game being played between soldiers and officers the day before the Battle of Bunker Hill. Baseball historian Priscilla Astifan discovered one such description, while researching her *Baseball In Rochester* (NY) history, in the following passage from an article titled "Continental Baseball" in an 1875 Spencerport, New York newspaper: "The student of American history will recollect that the day previous to the battle of Bunker Hill 'our boys' indulged in a friendly game of base ball. It may not be generally known that the return game was then and there arranged to be played at Spencerport [an outer Rochester suburb], September 11, 1875, at 2 PM, sharp." It goes on to refer to a ball that is large and round and other aspects of primitive baseball. It also mentions that "soarred" and "gousy" veterans elected themselves captains. Although it was not baseball as we know it today, it was still two teams, a ball, a bat, and bases. This was 64 years before Abner Doubleday's 'invention' of the game in 1839.

In the 1880s, in his later years, Whig politician Thurlow Weed reminisced of playing "base ball" in 1825 at "Mumford's meadow, by the side of the river above the falls," in Rochester, New York. Likewise, in *Grandfather Stories*, author Samuel Hopkins Adams reflects on going to his first ballgame in Rochester, New York, in the 1880s with his grandfather. An old ball player, his grandfather talks with a local fan about his playing days in Rochester in 1827. They played twelve men to a team at Mumford's Lot. Coincidence?

In 1886, a letter from Dr. Adam E. Ford recalls a ball game that he witnessed on June 4, 1838, in Beechville, Ontario. The following excerpts of this letter come from the *Journal of Sport History, Vol.15, No. 1 (Spring, 1988)*: " 'A Game of Long-Ago which Closely Resembled Our Present National Game'... The 4th of June, 1838 was a holiday in Canada, for the Rebellion of 1837 had been closed by the victory of the government over the rebels, and the birthday of His Majesty George the Fourth was set apart for general rejoicing. The chief event at the village of Beachville, in the County of Oxford, was a baseball match between the Beachville Club and the Zorras, a club hailing from the township of Zorra and North Oxford...

"The infield was a square, the base lines of which were twenty-four yards long, on which were placed five bags, thus . . . (See Beachvillle Diagram, page 11.)

"The distance from the thrower to the catcher was eighteen yards; the catcher standing three yards behind the home bye. From the home bye, or "knocker's" stone, to the first bye was six yards. The club (we had bats in cricket but we never used bats in playing base ball) was generally made of the best cedar, blocked out with an ax and finished on a shaving horse with a drawing knife. A wagon spoke, or any nice stick would do."

The game looked very close to what was called 'town ball' or the 'Massachusetts game,' with five 'byes' instead of four bases.

Why did teams from Rochester, New York and Beechville, Ontario play town ball, an organized game similar to the Massachusetts game? The upstate section of New York was once a part of Massachusetts—as late as 1791 when the Gorham/Phelps Act changed the states of New York and Massachusetts to their current alignment. That area of Ontario was known as Upper Canada. It came to be settled by Tories—those who were loyal to the King of England—who had come from New England. These same settlers may have played the English game of 'Rounders,' an early bat-and-ball game played as a children's game in England from the 1600s, in Massachusetts. So, it is widely believed that town ball and the Massachusetts game are direct descendants of that early English game; Rounders was Americanized long before Doubleday.

After the defeat of the Indian nations and the abandonment of their English allies in the Indian Wars of the late 1700s and the War of 1812, thus ending Indian resistance to western expansion into the region, people began to settle the Northwest Territory (now the Midwest) in hopes of finding land and fortune. What does this have to do with baseball in Chicago? It has to do with the expansion of baseball. Early Chicago settlers came from the East in great droves, thanks to the Erie Canal, St. Joseph River, and Lake Michigan. Americans and Canadians settled the Northwest Territory alike. So the early forms of baseball being played in Beechville and Rochester migrated to Chicago as the Tories and New Englanders traveled west, bringing their bat-and-ball games with them, planting the seeds of the National Pastime in the American Midwest.

In 1839, Chicago was a small, very raw city. As traders and merchants worked their daily jobs, how could they possibly have time to play base ball? Chances are they did make time. Though no proof exists of baseball being played in Illinois prior to 1851, there is proof that baseball traveled westward as people emigrated in the early decades of the 19th Century.

Extensive research into the early years of Chicago baseball history shows that as the city grew, the game grew with it. In this book you will find images perhaps not seen in 100 years, and information on Chicago baseball history that has never been discussed before. This includes early boxscores, early images of teams and players, and early stars of Chicago baseball. The professional game of baseball that we know today—the Cubs, the Sox—was formed long ago.

1830 CHICAGO. A picture of Chicago in 1830. Population 96. On the left bank of the Chicago River stands Fort Dearborn. In front of Fort Dearborn stands the Indian Agency House. On the right bank stands John Kinzie's house, known as Chicago's first permanent residence. In the distance near the fork in the river is Wolf's Point; the building standing there is Chief Alexander Robinson's House. Robinson was a Potawatomi whose father was Scottish and whose mother an Ottawa Indian from Green Bay. The Robinson House also became Chicago's first tavern. (From a lithograph in the collection of Historic Urban Plans, Ithaca, NY.)

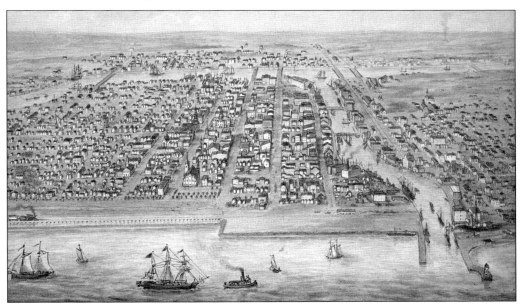

1857 CHICAGO. A picture of Chicago in 1853. Population 60,662. This lithograph shows the paradoxical view of young Chicago. As the city grew, you could still see the pastoral surroundings of the farmland on the outskirts. Chicago's first ball field, Union Grounds, was built just west of the fork in the Chicago River in 1856. The first team, known as the Union Base Ball Club, was aptly named after the grounds that they played on at Halsted and Harrison, which is where University of Illinois-Chicago sits today. (From a lithograph in the collection of Historic Urban Plans, Ithaca, NY)

THE GAME OF ROUNDERS. Notice the batter half way between the bases on the farthest base line and the stakes used for bases. Rounders was an early ancestor to baseball, played in England and brought to the states, possibly as early as the days of the pilgrims. (Photo Courtesy of Transcendental Graphics.)

DIAGRAM OF THE GAME PLAYED IN BEECHVILLE, ONTARIO. This diagram of the field discussed in Ford's 1838 Beechville game, with 21 yards between the bases, is the equivalent to modern day softball base dimensions. (Illustration Courtesy of Jack Freyer.)

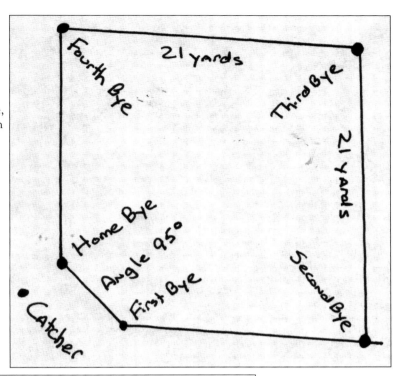

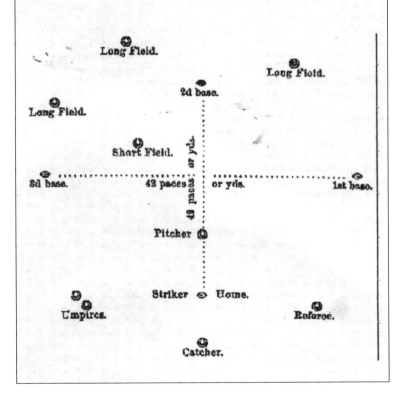

THE START OF THE MODERN GAME. The 1856 New York Putnam's laid out the image of the modern diamond, as seen in this 1856 Putnam Rules diagram. The game went from being played to 21 aces (runs) to its current format of nine innings. (Courtesy of Dean Thilgen and the Vintage Base Ball Association.)

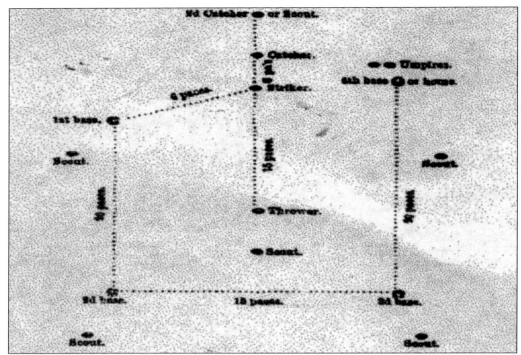

DIAGRAM OF THE EARLY GAME OF TOWN BALL (MASSACHUSETTS GAME). Town ball was played in rural America until the mid-1860s. Some towns still play the game in hamlets in the Appalachians. Its current version is called 'round-town' and is played to commemorate older towns' anniversaries in Virginia. (Courtesy of Dean Thilgen and the Vintage Base Ball Association.)

BAT & BALL PIONEERS. A group of children are depicted playing town ball. Town ball had unlimited players on defense, and players were put out by being hit with the ball. It's easy to see why the modern game took hold so quickly. (Courtesy of Transcendental Graphics.)

ONE

Chicago Baseball Archeology
1851–1869

As baseball spread across the Midwest, the 'national game' became increasingly popular in Chicago.

By the end of the 1850s, it was very apparent that organized baseball clubs were quickly developing in Chicago. In 1857, the Chicago Base Ball Association voted to adopt the Rules of the National Association of Base Ball Players. Those rules were a structured outgrowth of the New York Knickerbocker Rules, and will seem a bit peculiar to the modern day baseball fan. This meant that there were no balls or strikes; balls must be pitched underhand, not thrown, to the striker (batter); hit balls caught on the first 'bound' (bounce) were considered an out.

The quality of the game of base ball in those days was not always the best. No mitts were used, so 'muffs' (errors) were plentiful and games were typically high scoring. Keeping your opponent to fewer than ten runs was considered a defensive gem. The 'bound game' was in style until 1864, when top-level teams began to view the 'fly game' as the game of preference. The bound game was still played in 'muffin' games, however, as muffins were considered second-rate players.

Most base ball clubs consisted of 40-50 members, so that when no other competition was available, they could practice amongst themselves. It was at this time that the game became known as a "Gentleman's Game." Games in these days were social events. Clubs would play against each other for hours at a time, usually until the sun went down. When the early clubs played other clubs, a banquet usually followed with speeches given by the captains of each team. Praise went to those that deserved it. Good-natured ribbing was given to the players with 'muffin' quality in their game. Early newspaper accounts express surprise by the amount of female attendees to the games, "unlike any other of the sports."

Each club sported a 'first nine' and a 'second nine'—muffins typically played on the second nines. 'Picked nine' games were played for entertainment purposes, when players from multiple teams were put together to face a stronger opponent. On most of these occasions, the muffin game would be played, though this bound game would be virtually extinct at all levels by the end of the 1870s.

The earliest documented reference to Baseball in the state of Illinois is found in *Baseball in Old Chicago*, published by the Federal Writers Project in 1939. It cites *The Lockport Telegraph* reporting that on August 6th, 1851, the Hunkidoris of Joliet played the Sleepers of Lockport. The burgeoning towns of Lockport and Joliet, southwest of the City of Chicago, were developed in the 1820s, settled heavily by the Irish due to the construction of the Illinois & Michigan Canal. Both were very busy hubs in that era. Joliet in 1851 had a population that was just as large as Chicago. *The Lockport Telegraph* tells in a later edition of the newspaper that the Joliet team brought the "usual thugs and street Arabs" as fans.

The formal organization of teams with nicknames and references to an established fan base suggest that base ball had to be played in Chicago well before 1851. It would have been evolving for years. *Baseball in Old Chicago* also mentions the organization of a Union Base Ball Club in Chicago in 1856.

Of the newly developed Chicago teams, the Excelsior Club was the finest. In 1858, the Excelsiors established themselves as one of the first organized clubs in the city, and stayed together for a decade (though play was interrupted by the Civil War in 1861). Always up for a challenge, the Excelsior Club dominated the city baseball scene from 1859 to 1868. After they ran out of funds in 1869 and could find no sponsors, the city was without a top-level team for the 1869 season. This stirred outrage amongst city officials and businessmen, which led to the fielding of a professional nine for the 1870 season, the 'White Stockings' (discussed in Chapter Two).

From 1861 to 1864, very little ball was being played in the city, except at leisure. But the soldiers of the Civil War played day in and day out. They would use broomsticks and branches for bats. Rags sewn into a ball or a walnut wrapped in twine, any spherical object, would act as a ball. While writing home, a soldier in the Civil War named George Putnam mentioned, "Suddenly there came a scattering fire of which the three outfielders caught the brunt; the center field was hit and captured, the left and right field managed to get back into our lines. The attack... was repelled without serious difficulty, but we had not only lost our center field, but...the only baseball in Alexandria."

After the Civil War, the national game spread like wild fire. Teams popped up in places like California, New Orleans, Memphis and Minnesota. The war helped fan the hot coals of baseball's popularity, and by the mid-1860s, both the quality and the popularity of the game had increased. Teams traveled to tournaments and sought competition across the states, and the image of baseball, as we know it today, began its early growth.

Chicago and the Midwest (then considered the Northwest Territory) were quick to develop highly skilled teams. By 1865, the first regional associations were forming. Many state associations were already formed. Illinois and Michigan were the first to develop these associations in 1865. The Northwest Association is unique in that it was the first association outside of the New York Association to actively use members from a number of states. The Northwest Association set forth to establish regional tournaments and to spread the goodwill of the game in the Midwest.

In 1866, the first tournament of the Northwest Association was held in Rockford, Illinois. Attending teams included: Atlantic of Chicago (IL), Excelsior of Chicago (IL), Bloomington of Bloomington (IL), Cream City of Milwaukee (WI), Shaffer of Freeport (IL), Empire of Freeport (IL), Detroit of Detroit (MI), Forest City of Rockford (IL), Julian of Dubuque (IA), and Pecatonica of Pecatonica (IL).

The Excelsior Club of Chicago and the Detroit Club were considered the elite teams of the event. Chicago first had its hands full with a victory over the Empire team of Freeport, 26-24, before defeating Detroit, 16-10. The Excelsiors were to play the Bloomington, Illinois club for the championship, but Bloomington, being happy with second place, conceded the championship to the Excelsior Club.

In 1867, the Forest City Club of Rockford, which featured a young Albert Spalding and Ross Barnes—both future Chicago White Stockings stars—were the equal of, if not better than, the Excelsior Club. That season an East Coast base ball team attempted the first national tour. The National Club of Washington, D.C. toured the country, beating teams handily along the way. At the end of July 1867, the Nationals came to Chicago. Three games were scheduled over the course of five days. The Nationals would play the Forest City Club of Rockford, the Excelsior Club of Chicago, and the Atlantic Club of Chicago.

The Forest City Club, which had recently lost two matches to the Excelsiors (45-41 and 28-24), shocked the country by beating the Nationals 29-23 behind the stellar pitching of a teenage Al Spalding. Seeing this, the bettors went heavy on the Excelsiors for the next match. The Excelsiors were scored upon easily and often. They were soundly beaten 49-4 by the Nationals, prompting the press to cry scandal. These allegations were refuted several days later as the newspapers recanted and apologized for any wrongdoing. The Nationals went on to beat the Atlantics 78-17. The Excelsiors' loss to the Nationals was their only defeat of the year, as they finished with a 10-1 record.

In 1869, the National Association of Base Ball Players broke down their standings into two categories—Professional and Amateur. The best professional team that year was the Cincinnati Red Stockings, who went 57-0. The Rockford Forest City team, though still amateur in status, gave the Red Stockings a good run, losing 15-14. Rockford was 20-4 in 1869, better than any Chicago club. Chicago's elite team was the Athletics, who mustered a 7-4 mark for the year. By the end of 1869, the call went out in the Chicago papers to establish a professional team for 1870—which they did.

BEFORE BRICKS AND IVY. This is a woodcut of the Elysian Fields in Hoboken, New Jersey, c. 1857, from the sporting newspaper *Porter's Spirit of the Times*, predecessor of the more popular *Wilkes' Spirit of the Times*. The Elysian Fields were considered the incubator of the modern game of baseball. New York teams would cross the water to play at a more 'natural' setting. Note the shear magnificence of Mother Nature's stadium—the willows create a closed-in green cathedral. The game in progress is believed to be two New York teams, the Gothams and the Eagles. It is this game that would be adopted by the top-level Chicago clubs. (Courtesy of Dean Thilgen—Vintage Base Ball Association.)

EARLY CHICAGO CLUB. The first print mention of baseball in Chicago, dating to July of 1858, tells of a team called the Niagaras forming in the city. Early Chicago teams often took the names of popular East Coast teams, like the Atlantics and Excelsiors. The Federal Writers Project had claimed that the following passage was the oldest known mention of baseball being played: "The earliest newspaper report of a baseball game is found in the *Chicago Daily Journal* of August 17, 1858, which tells of a match game between the Unions and the Excelsiors to be played on August 19th." But this find predates the Federal Writers Project's by a month. (Courtesy of the Vintage Ballist; Research by Ted Hathaway of Rational Pastimes.)

(*above*) **A GENTLEMEN'S GAME.** Here is a description found in the Chicago Tribune of an 1858 match between a Chicago and a suburban team. Baseball in this time period was still a 'gentlemen's game.' (Courtesy of the Vintage Ballist; Research by Rational Pastimes.)

(*right*) **ADOPTION OF EAST COAST RULES.** The Chicago clubs adopted the 1857 rules of the National Association of Base Ball Players. Teams from around the country, which had organized to codify how baseball should be played, adopted these same rules. The National Association of Base Ball Players was the predominant force of early base ball. Its reign as the leading association in the country spanned from 1857 to 1870, when the National Association took the helm at the beginning of professionalism. (Courtesy of the Vintage Ballist; Research by Rational Pastimes.)

JIM CREIGHTON, BASE BALL'S FIRST STAR. Jim Creighton was the first innovator in the early game. Some researchers also conclude that Creighton was the first pitcher to use speed as a manner of getting a hitter out. In contrast to the gentleman's game, Creighton used a modern day "submarine" pitch to get batters out. Up until this time, the pitcher acted as a feeder, and the hitter could take ease in knowing that he would receive his pitch. Creighton, on the other hand, threw swiftly, moving the ball close to the striker's hands, much the same way modern pitchers throw, in hopes of getting a weak swing. Creighton was also a fine hitter and is rumored to have competed a full season with out getting a "hand out." Creighton died at the young age of 21, two days after rupturing an internal organ while hitting a home run in an Excelsior contest in 1861. (Courtesy of Transcendental Graphics.)

JAMES CREIGHTON,

DREADNAUGHT BASE BALL CLUB. These early Chicago players are watched by baseball's quickly growing fan-base.

EARLY BOX SCORE. The first recorded game of baseball played in Chicago, complete with box score, appeared in an 1859 edition of the Chicago Tribune. The primitive box score only featured runs. The Excelsior Club prevailed over the Atlantics, 31-17. (Courtesy of The Vintage Ballist; Research by Rational Pastimes.)

THE BASE BALL MATCH.—The "Excelsior" and "Atlantic" Clubs met on Saturday last and played their match on the grounds, corner of Washington and Sheldin streets. There were some five hundred spectators, not a few of whom were ladies. The day was pleasant, the game excellently played and the occasion one that was was generally enjoyed, and we hope to see such matches frequently played. We give the score:

ATLANTIC.		EXCELSIOR.	
E. Van Buren, c.	1	W. Hartshorne, 1st b	4
A. L. Adams, p.	1	M. F. Prouty, c	6
B. Burton, 1st b	2	J. Malcolm, p	6
G. Childs, 2nd b	1	J. A. Hays, 3rd b	1
W. Scates, 3rd b	2	S. Farwell, 2nd b	6
C. Scates, l. f.	2	Dr. Hunt, r. f	3
F. F. Burton, r. f.	4	W. Houghton, c. f	3
E. Bean, l. f.	2	G. C. Smith, l. f.	1
S. Child, c. f	2	F. H. Bostock, s. f.	3
Total	17	Total	31

EARLY GAME OF BASE BALL. This print, *c.* 1859, shows what the above match between the Excelsior Club and the Atlantics would likely have looked like—with "some five hundred spectators, not a few of whom were ladies" lining the outfield. (Courtesy of Transcendental Graphics.)

BASE BALL IN CHICAGO

BASE BALL IN CHICAGO.—An exceedingly well played match took place in that city on the 27th ult., between the Excelsior and Columbia clubs, the former giving the odds of a man. This did not prevent them from gaining the victory, however, by a large majority, their score at the close being 49 to 33. The particulars of the play are contained in the annexed summary:

EXCELSIOR. NAMES.	H. L.	RUNS.	COLUMBIA. NAMES.	H. L.	RUNS.
Hunt, 3d base	2	8	Gilespie, catcher	3	5
Malcom, pitcher	5	3	Jauncey, pitcher	1	5
Smith, left field	5	4	G Simonds, 1st base	4	3
Prouty, first base	4	6	Varian, short	2	4
Farwell, right field	3	6	E Simonds, 3d base	5	2
Nichols, catcher	1	9	J H Lee, right field	3	4
Ousterhout; 2d base	5	5	Saunders, left field	5	2
Bostock, short stop	2	8	G T Lee, centre field	2	4
			King, 6 in 2d b	1	2
			Davis, 3 in	1	2
Total		49	Total		33

RUNS MADE IN EACH INNINGS.

	1st.	2d.	3d.	4th.	5th.	6th.	7th.	8th.	9th.
Excelsior	8	2	14	4	5	5	4	5	3
Columbia	1	5	4	0	2	2	4	12	3

HOW PUT OUT.

EXCELSIOR.	B'nd.	Base.	Fly.	COLUMBIA.	B'nd.	Base.	Fly.
Nichols	13	0	2	Gilespie	5	1	0
Hunt	0	3	0	Jauncey	1	0	0
Smith	1	0	1	G Simonds	4	0	0
Farwell	2	0	0	Varian	0	0	0
Prouty	0	3	0	E Simonds	2	1	0
Ousterhout	1	0	0	J H Lee	1	0	1
Bostock	0	0	0	Saunders	4	0	0
Malcom	1	0	0	G T Lee	1	2	1
				King	0	0	0

Balls Passed—Gilespie 6, G. Simmonds 7, Nichols 6.
Hunt and Nichols each made one home run.
Umpire—W. B. Willard, of Olympic Club.

NO PITCHERS DUEL. The Excelsiors dominated, defeating the Columbia team with a 49-33 victory. This box score comes from the *New York Clipper*, 1859. Thanks to Henry Chadwick, the *Clipper* was the leading base ball paper of the day. If you look closely at this boxscore, you can get a clear sense of what happened that day and how the defense played. Though it was well over a hundred years ago, we see that the catcher was the main defender and usually the best athlete on the team. (Courtesy of the Vintage Ballist; Research by Rational Pastimes.)

BALL PLAY. 9/3/1859

BASE BALL IN CHICAGO.—A well played match between the first nines of the Atlantic and Excelsior took place on the 15th ult., for the championship. The game was closely contested throughout and was won by the former. The Atlantics went into the field believing they were to be beaten, but determined to reduce their defeat as much as possible. The Excelsiors worked hard, and in the 9th innings smilingly took the bat to make three runs—all that was needed—but bad play prevented them making any. There was a large crowd present, who cheered lustily at the termination of the match. The victorious club only started this spring, and played the Excelsiors some time since to learn the game, but were beaten almost 2 to 1. They have now beaten the Excelsiors two out of the three games played, which entitles them to the championship. Success to them. The score was as follows:

EXCELSIOR. NAMES.	H. L.	RUNS.	ATLANTIC. NAMES.	H. L.	RUNS.
Malcom, pitcher	2	4	Van Buren, jr, catcher	4	1
Rounds, 2d base	5	0	Adams, pitcher	2	2
Nichols, catcher	4	1	O'Neil, 1st base	3	3
Smith, left field	3	1	T Burton, 2d base	0	6
Prouty, 1st base	4	1	B Burton, 3d base	3	3
Kennedy, centre field	1	3	Sylvester, right field	4	1
Hunt, 3d base	4	3	Childs, centre field	5	0
Bostock, right field	1	3	Barrett, left field	3	1
Pickard, short stop	3	2	Scates, short stop	3	1
Total		16	Total		18

RUNS MADE IN EACH INNINGS.

	1st	2d	3d	4th	5th	6th	7th	8th	9th
Atlantic	2	2	5	0	1	0	3	3	
Excelsior	1	5	2	1	3	0	4	0	0

HOW PUT OUT.

EXCELSIOR.	Fly.	B'nd.	Base.	T'tl.	ATLANTIC.	Fly.	B'nd.	Base.	T'tl.
Malcom	2	0	1	3	Van Buren	12	0	0	12
Rounds	0	0	0	0	Adams	0	1	1	2
Nichols	8	0	1	9	O'Neil	0	6	1	7
Smith	2	0	0	2	T Burton	0	1	0	1
Prouty	0	5	0	5	B Burton	1	0	0	1
Kennedy	0	0	1	1	Sylvester	0	0	0	0
Hunt	1	2	1	4	Childs	1	0	0	1
Bostock	2	0	0	2	Barrett	3	0	0	3
Pickard	0	1	0	1	Scates	0	0	0	0
Total	16	8	3	27	Total	17	8	2	27

Umpire, E. H. Quimby.

CHICAGO'S FIRST CHAMPS. By reading this article from the September 3, 1859 *Chicago Tribune*, we gather that the Atlantics seemingly won the first match. This match, won by the Atlantics 18-16, gave them the first city championship. (Courtesy of the *Vintage Ballist*.)

EARLIEST GAME PHOTO. This 1861 photo of baseball, left, and cricket fields, right, could be the earliest photo of a game. It would have resembled the games described in the boxscores on the opposite page. (Taken from a Princeton College Class Album, Courtesy of Transcendental Graphics.)

THE FLY GAME. This 1860's cigar label depicts the "Fly Game," which came in vogue at the beginning of 1864 when it was adopted as the 'professional' game by the National Association of Base Ball Players. (Photo courtesy of Transcendental Graphics)

LINCOLN VS. DOUGLASS. An example of recreation games included a match played in Chicago between Douglas and Lincoln staffers. The Douglas Camp won the match 16-14, but Lincoln went on to win the election. The hard-to-read quote on the bottom of this clipping has Lincoln saying, "Never mind, there's a victory in store where Douglas will make no 'runs.' He is a lame 'short stop,' and has been 'caught out.'" This ancient boxscore is from *Henry Chadwick's Scrapbook*. Chadwick invented the boxscore as we know it. (Courtesy of the *Vintage Ballist*.)

LINCOLN THE BALL PLAYER. Lincoln was known to be very fond of the game. It is rumored that he played ball on the back lawn of the White House with his son, before his son passed away at an early age. It has also been said that Lincoln was a "sound batsman." (Courtesy of Transcendental Graphics.)

THE NATIONAL GAME. THREE "OUTS" AND ONE "RUN".
ABRAHAM WINNING THE BALL.

CIVIL WAR CAMP GAME. This is a lithograph of a game being played in prison camp in Salisbury, North Carolina, in 1864. It is scenes like this that led historians to believe that the spread of baseball was a product of the Civil War. Prisoners from everywhere would pass the days playing ball, even against their captors. The National Association's greatest growth came in the years following the Civil War, eventually giving way to professionalism in the 1870s. (Photo courtesy of Transcendental Graphics)

THE GREAT NATIONAL GAME.

OUR COLORED BROTHER. "HI YAH! STAN' BACK DAR; IT'S DIS CHILE'S INNIN'S NOW."

NATIONAL GAME. The "Great National Game" as depicted in *Harper's Weekly* in 1865, shortly after the Emancipation Proclamation. (Photo Courtesy of Transcendental Graphics.)

BASE BALL CONVENTION IN CHICAGO.

ORGANIZATION OF A NORTHWESTERN ASSOCIATION.

Base Ball appears to be growing more and more popular; it has evidently become one of our "peculiar institutions." On the 6th inst., about twenty-five delegates from various Northwestern clubs assembled in Chicago, and formed what is to be known as the "Northwestern Association of Base Ball Players." After organizing the convention, a committee was appointed to draft a constitution and by-laws. The committee reported as follows:—

WHEREAS, The superiority and growing interest of the national game of base ball in the West, and the distance and difficulty of representation in the base ball clubs of the East, are such, that the interests of base ball demand a separate convention in the West; therefore, be it

Resolved, That we, the members of clubs in the States of the West, organize ourselves into a Convention, to be known as the "National Association of Base Ball Players of the West."

The Committee also suggest that we adopt the rules and regulations of the National Association of Base Ball Players, held in New York city on the 14th of December, 1864, subject to such amendments as the said Convention may adopt at their meeting to be held in Buffalo on the 18th of the present month—with the exception of not admitting members under eighteen years of age. It is also suggested that the officers of the Association consist of a President, Vice-President, Secretary and Treasurer. The report was accepted and adopted.

The following officers were then elected to serve for the ensuing year:—President, G. O. Smith, of Chicago; Vice-President, T. G. read, of Laporte, Ind.; Secretary, E. H. Griss, of Rockfork, Ill.; Treasurer, R. H. Anderson, of Detroit.

At this point an amendment was made in the appointment of an Assistant Vice-President and Corresponding Secretary from each State. The list of officers, as appointed by the President, was as follows:—

State.	Vice-President.	Cor. Sec'y.
Indiana	A. Brewer	L. C. Patrick.
Michigan	Hy. Burroughs	B. Ives.
Illinois	A. M. Kenzie	G. E. King.
Missouri	G. Kilpatrick	J. H. Reed.
Iowa	J. DeLangworthy	B. M. Harger.
Ohio	J. J. McCook	B. R. Hayett.
Wisconsin	M. Treadway	G. B. Hopkins.
Minnesota	J. H. Gibbens	R. O. Olm.

The rules of the game of base ball, as fixed by the National Association, were adopted. The title of the Association was amended by the insertion of "Northwestern" instead of the "National." It was resolved that it should be the duty of every club in the association to report to the Corresponding Secretary all match games in which they might be engaged, and that he report said games to the Secretary of the Association. After some business of minor importance, the Convention adjourned to meet again on the first Wednesday after the annual meeting of the National Base Ball Association in 1866.

OUR PECULIAR INSTITUTION. This article from *Wilkes Spirit of the Times* announces the first meeting of the Northwestern Association. Teams started playing regionally, thanks to the barnstorming going on in the East. (Courtesy of the *Vintage Ballist*.)

BASE-BALL MATTERS.

THE GRAND BASE-BALL TOURNAMENT.

TEN CLUBS ON THE GROUND.

GREAT ATTENDANCE AND EXCITING GAMES.

FIRST DAY.

ROCKFORD, Ill., June 26.

The long-looked-forward-to base-ball tournament of the northwest commenced in this city yesterday. The clans gathered strong. Ten clubs mustered their nines in Rockford's hostelries. For the nonce bat and ball are omnipresent and captains omnipotent.

A noble set of young men, vigorous, healthy, athletic, fitted for honorable contentions are these base-ball players, these contestants in the national ball game of the United States. All in the prime of life, at that period when mere existence is most a pleasure, they are eager for the fray, for the skirmish at the field—the field of the ball and the bat. Ten noble bands of young men that would do honor to any letter, represent the best blood of their respective cities; the very essence of athletic manhood. Base-ball playing has done this for them; made them what they are; given them a means of healthful, invigorating recreation. And they love this game which has done so much for them with all the ardor of youth. About it they are enthusiastic and never tire in its praise. And long may it be so! What better could supply its place?

Rockford has been well chosen for the contests of these favorite clubs of the northwest. It is a beautiful, orderly, clean little city, of perhaps 10,000 or 12,000 inhabitants, and has welcomed warmly the nines to her homes.

The spot chosen for the field of play covers four acres of the county fair grounds. The in-field is all that can be desired—smooth and clear of trees and other obstacles to the progress of ball and man; but the out-field is badly disfigured, in a base-ball point of view, by trees. On the whole, however, the grounds are as good as could be expected, if not as good as could be desired, and are within a short distance, about half a mile, from the city. The following are the prizes:

The Norman Prize: 1st, a magnificent gold ball, regulation-size, for the beating club in the tournament; 2nd, a beautiful gold-mounted rosewood bat, for the second best club.

3d. The Rockford Register Prize, by the Editors of the Rockford *Register:* A silver ball and a silver-mounted bat for the third best club, or to be awarded as may be directed by the captains of the contesting clubs.

4th. Holland House Prize: A silver pitcher to the best thrower.

5th. White's Hotel Prize: A silver goblet to the second best thrower.

6th. American House Prize: A splendid silver-mounted belt to the quickest runner of bases.

7th. Auctioneer's Prizes—by J. M. Hodge, 48 State Street: A silver tea-sett, or $30 in money, to the most graceful playing club, to be determined by a committee of ladies, selected by the Superintendent.

8th. Rock River Insurance Company Prize, by the employees of the Company: A silver ice pitcher and goblets.

LADIES' PRIZES.—9th. By the ladies of the East side: A magnificent bouquet to the best batsman. 10th. By the ladies of the West side. A splendid floral wreath, to the player making the most home-runs.

11th. Chandler & Humphrey's Prize—to the worst beaten club. Prize to be awarded on the ground.

THE CONTESTANTS.

The following is a list of the clubs present: Atlantic, Chicago; Excelsior, Chicago; Bloomington, Bloomington; Cream City, Milwaukie, Wis.; Shaffer. Freeport, Ill.; Empire, Freeport, Ill.; Detroit, Detroit, Forest City, Rockford, Ill.; Julian, Dubuque, Iowa; Pecatonica, Pecatonica, Ill.

THE PROGRAMME.

At a meeting of the captains of the respective nines at the Holland House this morning, the clubs were arranged by ballot to play as follows

TUESDAY.—Forenoon: Detroit vs. Pecatonica. Afternoon: Bloomington vs. Atlantic.

WEDNESDAY.—Forenoon: Julian vs. Cream City. Afternoon: Shaffer vs. Forrest City.

THURSDAY.—Forenoon: Excelsior vs. Empire City.

THE PLAYING.

About 10½ o'clock this morning the various clubs proceeded to the grounds where the tournament was to be held. The weather was fine cloudy, and consequently cool. Sol's rays to ardent gazers were intercepted by the cloud's draperies, and the breeze kept the air delightfully cool and bracing, although it somewhat varied the straight line and the distance which the balls, impelled by the sturdy arms of the batsmen were meant to pursue.

A goodly throng of admirers, dotted here and there with fair ones, encircled the batsman's half of the ground, and, by their charms, moved the players to do credit to themselves and the clubs which they represented.

THE FIRST MATCH.

The first match of the tournament was between the Pecatonica and Detroit Clubs.

OUR FIRST TOURNAMENT. The first tournament in the State of Illinois was announced in the *Chicago Tribune* in 1866. Awards were given for stellar individual play, as well as team play. (Courtesy of the *Vintage Ballist*; Research by Rational Pastimes.)

27

The principal and most exciting match of the day was that between the Empire club, of Freeport, and the Excelsior club, of Chicago. To witness these two rival clubs—rivals in reputation—who have fought together, and who, to-day, come together, with a full determination to do their best, a large crowd of people, among whom was a liberal sprinkling of ladies, lined the playing grounds, and lent their cheers to the occasion. The following is the score:

EMPIRE.	O.	R.	EXCELSIOR.	O.	R.
Butler, l f	2	5	Stearns, c	1	6
Farwell, 3d b	3	4	Foley, 3d b	1	5
Lightheart, r f	3	4	Thompson, l f	3	3
Best. p	3	3	O. Berlander, 2d b	3	2
Buckmow, 1st b	2	1	Kennedy, p	2	2
Brewster, c f	2	2	Budd, r f	5	0
Stoekopf, 2d b	6	0	McNally, 1st b	5	1
Thomas, c	3	2	Goodrich, c f	2	3
Kavanagh, s s	3	3	Dean, s s	2	4

RUNS IN EACH INNING.

	1st.	2d.	3d.	4th.	5th.	6th.	7th.	8th.	9th.
Empire	3	3	7	0	6	0	2	0	3—24.
Excelsior	2	4	0	8	1	3	5	3	0—26.

THE PRINCIPAL MATCH. The great match of the 1866 tournament was between the Empire Team of Freeport, Illinois and the Excelsior Club of Chicago. As can be seen in this Chicago Tribune boxscore, these two rivals did not disappoint the large crowd in attendance. (Courtesy of the *Vintage Ballist*; Research by Rational Pastimes.)

THE 1866 ROCKFORD FOREST CITY CLUB.

1866 TOURNAMENT CHAMPS. The *Chicago Tribune* posted this championship notice of the 1866 Northwest Tournament with a glowing review of the skill and comportment of all participants. (Courtesy of the *Vintage Ballist*; Research by Rational Pastimes.)

CHICAGO vs. DETROIT.—Now comes on the game that shall stir the hearts of base-ball players and rouse them to unwonted enthusiasm; the Excelsior, of Chicago, and the Detroit, of Detroit. Is it not a worthy duel? They are well known, and need no praise. Admirers and spectators line the grounds in a way that they have not done before. Read the names of the illustrious nines—the men that Detroit and Chicago are proud to call their own.

The game commenced at 2:40 P. M., the Detroit going to bat first. It was well opened by J. W. Sternes catching a foul in the fly, in fine style, which was followed in rapid succession by another catch, equally good, by the 1st base man, Goodrich, the Excelsiors thus catching two out in the very beginning of the game. Van Norman sent a ball flying over into the right field, which was magnificently caught by Budd, who thereby astonished his friends.

In the second inning, a tremendous hit is made by Phelps, and the ball whizzes through the air with a rapidity and force as if it would pierce anything that came across its course; but the short stop is there, and the ball finds it way into his hands, and makes no more impression, apparently, than would a feather descending in the same.

The Excelsiors fight well, are careful, seize every opportunity, do good fielding, and splendid throwing and catching. Thus they try the skill of the Detroiters, the favorites on the grounds, and whitewash them in three successive innings, the fifth, sixth, and seventh. In the eighth inning the Detroit made one and Excelsiors seven, the largest score made in the game. This made the Excelsiors six ahead of the Detroit club, and the latter being whitewashed in their ninth inning, admitted themselves beat. The following were the winning nine (Excelsiors), in a score of 16 against 10: Sternes, Folley, Thompson, Oberlander, Kennedy, Budd, McNalley, Goodrich, and Dean. Time, three hours and thirty minutes.

ALBERT GOODWILL SPALDING. Al Spalding started pitching at the tender age of 14 for the Forest City Club of Rockford. During the next three decades, Spalding would make a mark on the game like no other man. He was pivotal as a player, a coach, a founding member of the National League, and, finally, as a publisher and sporting goods dealer. He was the star pitcher for the 1876 Champion Chicago White Stockings. (Courtesy of the *Vintage Ballist*.)

EXCELSIOR.	O.	R.	FOREST CITY.	O.	R.
Stearns, c.	3	3	Adda, 2d b.	1	5
McNally, p.	4	3	Barnes, s. s.	4	2
Kennedy, 1st b.	2	4	King, c.	4	3
Oliver, 2d b.	4	3	Spalding, p.	3	3
Foley, 3d b.	2	5	Barker, c. f.	0	4
Alston, s. s.	3	4	Lighthart, 3d b.	3	2
Oberlander, r. f.	3	2	Wheeler, l. f.	5	1
Budd, l. f.	4	2	Buckman, 1st b.	3	3
Blakslee, c. f.	3	2	Starr, r. f.	4	2

RUNS MADE IN EACH INNING.

	1st.	2d.	3d.	4th.	5th.	6th.	7th.	8th.	9th.	
Excelsiors	6	4	0	2	0	5	10	1	0	28
Forest City	2	1	10	2	2	0	2	4	2	25

Umpire—Mr. Fred. Callaway, late of the Eurekas. Scorers—Messrs. Cleveland and Burns. Time of game—Three hours and forty minutes.

A GRAND MATCH. On the 4th of July 1867, a grand match was played between the Excelsior Club of Chicago and Spalding's Forest City Club of Rockford. The Excelsiors were the reigning champions of the Northwest Association. The Forest City Club was one of the finest teams of the day, featuring players like Al Spalding, Ross Barnes, and Bobby Addy—all of whom would go on to star for the Chicago Whitestockings of the National League in the 1870s. Still, as this boxscore from *Henry Chadwick's Scrapbook* proves, the talented Excelsiors were victorious over Spalding and the Rockford team in a close match, 28-25. (Courtesy of the *Vintage Ballist*.)

ROSCOE "ROSS" BARNES. Ross Barnes was the master of the "fair-foul hit." The "fair/foul" hit was a hit that hit fair then went foul. Because of the quirky nature of this rule, some skilled batsmen would purposely hit the ball down hard in fair territory with the hopes of it bounding foul. This play was virtually impossible to defend against. Barnes started his career with the Forest City Club of Rockford and finished with the Chicago Whitestockings. Once the fair-foul rule was abolished in 1877, his career quickly deteriorated.

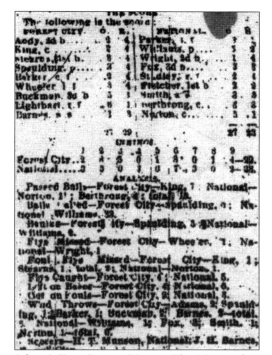

(*above*) **THE GREAT UPSET.** The National Club of Washington was undefeated on their 1867 tour until they ran into a young pitcher names Al Spalding.

(*right*) **AN ALLEGED SCANDAL.** The much-anticipated game between the undefeated Excelsiors versus the once-defeated Nationals generated quite a bit of interest—and wagering. Earlier in the month, the Excelsiors beat the Forest City Club 28-25. And the Forest City Club had just defeated the Nationals. All bets sided on the Excelsiors. As you can see by the outcome, many people lost their money. It was speculated that the Excelsiors "threw the game," but it was never proven. This Chicago Tribune boxscore shows that the match was not even close, the Nationals dominating the premier Chicago team, 49-4. (Courtesy of the *Vintage Ballist*.)

GRAND TOUR OF THE NATIONAL CLUB.

THE NINTH MATCH.—THE GREAT VICTORY OF THE TOUR—DEFEAT OF THE CHAMPIONS OF THE WEST—We have witnessed many a brilliant exhibition of the beauties of base-ball in our experience, but we never saw a finer display than that made by the Nationals in their match with the Excelsiors of Chicago, the champion club of the West, which took place at Dexter Park, July 27th, in the presence of the largest, most respectable, and orderly assemblage of spectators we have ever known to be at a base-ball match. The circumstances attendant upon this contest were peculiar. In the first place, the inglorious defeat of the Nationals by the Rockford Club had led the Chicago people to underestimate the abilities of the National nine, and fully to expect a triumph for their champion nine, especially as the Excelsiors had twice this season defeated the Rockford Club. Secondly, the National nine proper had not yet played in a match this season, the series of the tour being experimental contests to train the nine to meet the strong clubs of the East; and thirdly, the defeat sustained had to be offset by a victory which would, at one and the same time, prove that the National nine were capable of better play than that shown in any previous game of the tour, and that, when properly placed, each man in his right position, they could develope their full strength, and play a game the strongest club in the country would find it hard to beat.

The sting of defeat is always a strong incentive to extra exertion, when sustained by manly players; but, in this instance, the boastful comments of the Chicago press formed an additional motive for an earnest effort to wipe off the blot upon their escutcheon. It turned out, the editorials upon the superior prowess of Western clubs, and the rather blatant comments on the "easy thing" the Chicago clubs had to conquer the club which had defeated those of every other Western city, were rather premature; the result of the contest, which, in the estimation of the Chicago editors, was to be the crowning triumph of the tour, actually making their own editorials the most pointed articles against them which could have been penned. One of them—that in the Chicago *Times*—alluded to the defeat of the Nationals, by stating that, if the club would remain a while in Chicago, inhale the Lake breezes, the Excelsior Club, and learn to play ball, they might, in time, hope to win a trophy from the great club of the West. Of course, this talk now becomes rich in sarcasm, and these self same editorials are now the laughing-stock of the city. Unfortunately, however, for the credit of the Chicago press, the braggadocio over the Rockford Club's success was followed by gross abuse of the National Club, when the local pride of the Lake City was taken down by the overwhelming defeat of the pet club of Chicago. The old song says, "Where'er you find the judgment weak, the prejudice is strong," and the editorial comments on the Excelsior match practically illustrated the fact. Moreover, the self-same spirit which dictates undue exultation over a fallen foe, is the same from which emanates the injustice and rancor of partizan disappointment; and this fact, too, the *Tribune* and the *Republican* editorials fully proved; for, after boasting over the victory of the third day so excessively, they charged the defeat of the Excelsiors to causes as justly attributable to the President of the National Club by the editorials in question, which we give below, suffice to explain the matter, and, without further preface, we proceed to describe this grand match and splendid victory of the National Club.

The weather on the occasion was all that could have been desired; for, though the sun was hot, a cool breeze made the atmosphere pleasant. The grounds, too, were livelier than on Thursday, and the immense crowd were kept back in their places, the entire field being encircled before the game was half through, and the outer circle was not far from a mile in circumference. For the first time, the Nationals presented their nine in their right positions, with George Wright at short field, Robinson at left, and Parker at second. The game began at 2:20 P.M., with the Nationals at the bat, and as their first two strikers retired in succession, it looked as if a second defeat was to mark the game; but this time George Wright came to the rescue in earnest, and, hitting a good one to right field, opened play in base running, and, as the others followed suit well at the bat until Parker again came to the bat, no less than seven runs were scored, Williams being the third hand out. The Nationals now went to the field, and their countenances displayed that this time they were earnestly bent upon doing the very best to win, and by the fine fielding of balls by Fox and Parker to Fletcher, the Excelsiors were disposed of for a blank, one man being left on his third, the tally of the first inning being 7 to 0 in favor of the Nationals. In the second inning the Nationals added 5 to their score, and again caused their opponents to draw a blank, a splendid running catch by Berthrong and a beauty by Norton marking the fielding—tally, 12 to 0.

In the third inning the Excelsiors scored two by good batting, after the Nationals had demoralized them by running up a score of 21 against them; but afterward, splendid fielding by the National men, in which all took part, caused their retirement for blank scores, the Nationals in the interim running up their score to 47, the tally at the close of the sixth inning being 47 to 2. Thus far, the play of the Nationals, both at the bat and in the field, had been a model display, not an error marking the play of a member of the nine. Afterward, though they still fielded admirably, two or three errors crept in, and the Excelsiors thereby added two more runs to their score, good hits also helping them materially. This also improved in their fielding very much, they keeping the score of the Nationals down to single, one blank also being scored; the totals at the close of the ninth inning standing at 49 to 4 in favor of the Nationals. The prevailing impression at the close of this contest, among the greater portion of those who had witnessed the Rockford game, was, that that defeat had been purposely sustained. The following is the score:

NATIONAL.	O.	R.	EXCELSIOR.	O.	R.
Parker, 2d b	5	2	Stearns, c	3	1
Williams, p	5	4	McNally, p	3	0
Wright, s s	1	8	Kennedy, 2d b	3	1
Robinson, l f	5	5	Budd, l f	3	0
Fox, 3d b	3	7	Willard, s s	2	1
Fletcher, 1st b	2	6	Falley, 3d b	4	0
Norton, c	3	6	Blakeslee, c f	2	1
Studley, r f	1	6	Barker, 1st b	4	0
Berthrong, c f	2	5	Oberland, r f	3	0

RUNS MADE IN EACH INNING.

	1st.	2d.	3d.	4th.	5th.	6th.	7th.	8th.	9th.	
National	7	5	21	5	1	8	1	0	1	—49
Excelsior	0	0	2	0	0	0	1	0	1	—4

Umpire—Mr. Dietrich, of the Bloomington Club. Scorers—Messrs. Munson and Cleveland. Time of Game—Three hours and thirty minutes. The umpiring was excellent, and the utmost good feeling prevailed throughout the game.

In the evening, the National Club visited McVicker's Theatre by invitation, and the victors were the cynosure of all eyes.

The Nationals challenged the Forest City Club to play a return game

THE CHAMPS. The Cincinnati Red Stockings featuring Harry and George Wright handily won the 1868 'Championship of the West'. The 1869 Red Stockings team, pictured here, went on to an undefeated 57-0 season. The 1869 Red Stockings were considered the first "professional" team. Each player was paid a minimum of $1500 for his services. The Red Stockings' George and Harry Wright were given the order to put the best team money could buy on the field. Almost every professional player in the Midwest was lured away from the East Coast, because that's where the greatest talent was. The 1870 White Stockings were a direct result of Chicago officials seeing what the Cincys did, and then copying the idea of using professional players. (Courtesy of David Rudd and Cycleback Press.)

TWO

The National Association
1870–1875

The 1870s marked the end of amateur baseball and the beginning of the new professional era. Since the unrivaled success of the openly professional Red Stockings the previous season, more and more big cities were compelled to follow Cincinnati's footsteps and field an all-professional ball club. Once team owners figured out how to make money, the larger city team owners took full advantage of the situation. In 1870, Chicago was no exception. The Chicago Base Ball Club (later known as the White Stockings because of their uniforms) became the first professional team of paid players to field a team in Chicago.

In the fall of 1869, the Chicago team put an ad calling for top-level players in the then-popular sports weekly the *New York Clipper*. They also sent team Captain Tom Foley on a recruiting trip out east. This helped the team attract topnotch talent like Levi Meyerle and Ned Cuthbert (who is widely credited with the first 'slide') from the Philadelphia Athletics; Ed Pinkham, James Wood, Fred Treacey, and Charlie Hodes from the Brooklyn Eckfords; and Bub McAtee and Clipper Flynn, who had played with the Lansingburgh Unions. Among the new players on the Chicago roster, only Ed Duffy had not played on a "pro" team in 1869, because of blacklisting for his role in a thrown game while playing for the New York Mutuals in 1865. Pilfering players from established pro teams made Chicago a top five team along with Cincinnati, Philadelphia, Boston, and New York in 1870.

Amateur teams and professional teams both competed in the National Association in 1870, and the disparity of talent is reflected in the box scores. The Chicago club, leading the schedule against amateur teams, started the season 31-0. In back-to-back games, Chicago pounded the Bluff City team of Memphis, Tennessee, 157-1, and a few days later beat the Grove City team of Kankakee, Illinois, 111-5. The team finished 65-8 overall and 22-7 against other professionals, giving them the best record in the country.

On November 1, Chicago played the New York Mutuals for the outright championship of the country. The two teams had split four games during the regular season. In a closely contested game, the Mutuals, who were leading 13-12 in the ninth inning, pulled their team off of the field in protest over bad umpiring and unruly fans. The score was then reverted backed to the eighth inning, which had Chicago ahead, 7-5. To this day, naturally, New Yorkers feel that they won and Chicagoans think that Chicago won.

In 1871, the National Association became a true professional league. The Chicago White Stockings, the Boston Red Stockings, and the Philadelphia Athletics were the strongest of the nine professional teams. Other pro teams of that season included the New York Mutuals, Washington Olympics, Troy Haymakers, Rockford Forest Citys, Cleveland Forest Citys, and Fort Wayne Kekiongas.

On October 8, 1871, the Great Chicago Fire wiped out the White Stockings' ballpark, Lake Park, which was on Randolph and Michigan. And with the ballpark went the team's equipment and uniforms. In first place at the time, Chicago limped into a championship game on October 30 in Brooklyn to face the Philadelphia Athletics. The Athletics won 4-1 and clinched the pennant. Chicago did not field a team again until 1874.

The White Stocking teams of 1874-75 were made up of stars from the 1860s. The White Stockings were fairly competitive, but never climbed above .500 in either of these two years. Davy Force and Levi Meyerle led this makeshift team. Davy Force was a fine fielder and decent with the bat, but he will go down in history as the main reason why William Hulbert decided to start the National League. Force had signed a contract for the 1875 season with the White Stockings, only to renege and sign with the Philadelphia Athletics. When the National Association ruled in favor of the Athletics, William Hulbert vowed for revenge. He got it when the National League was formed in 1876.

Just as baseball was in transition from the amateur to the professional game, the manufacture and sale of baseball equipment was becoming a big business in itself. In this article from an 1870 Chicago Tribune, Henry Chadwick gives his strong opinions on things such as quality and playability of different equipment on the market:

> In relation to material now used in playing base ball, a few hints will not be out of place. Some dispute has arisen of late in regard to the ball, it being claimed that the Atlantic Club of Brooklyn use what has only lately been termed an "elastic" ball, and which is no more nor less than a Ross or Van Horn ball, both being very lively, and made strictly in accordance with the regulations, being 5¹/4 ounces in weight, 9¹/4 inches in circumference, and composed of yarn and India rubber, covered with sheepskin. These balls sell in this city for ____ and $1.75 respectively. It is optional with nines to use them. They are better for the batters than the fielders. The balls known as Atlantic or Bounding Rock, may now be deemed "dead;" that is, they are not so lively—will not bound so high—as the Ross or Van Horn, although they are made according to the requirements of the association. They can be purchased for $1.50 each and are the favorites for practice and amateur matches. In addition to these are the Harwood, Peck and Snyder, Junior, Diamond, and practice balls at $1 and 75¢ each. The ball of the New York Rubber Company is a failure for base ball uses, the rubber covers tearing off easily. It is really an "elastic" dead ball.

After similarly discussing the merits of various bats, bases and uniforms, Chadwick informs local 'baseballists' of where they can find such goods:

> Base ball clubs and players can find everything they desire at the Chicago Base Ball Emporium of J.W.D. Kelley & Bro. No. 164 Lake St. West of LaSalle. This is ball headquarters for the West and the ____ of the several hundred ball players can be found registered there. The Messrs. Kelley have already fitted several city clubs with handsome uniforms, and are amply prepared to fill large or small orders for base ball goods.

Another interesting development in the early 1870s was the organization of the first black teams. The earliest known organized black team was the Pythian Club of Philadelphia. It has been recorded that they first played as early as 1867. Chicago was not far behind. In Peter Morris' book, *Baseball Fever, Early Baseball in Michigan*, he discusses the cancellation of a game by a touring black team from Chicago, the Uniques in 1874. Although nothing else has been found at the time of printing of this book, it does shed light on the fact that black baseball was organized far sooner than originally thought. Until recently, the 1880s were believed to be the starting point of Negro league teams.

As the National Association faded, the rise of professionalism and the rise of base ball went hand in hand. The transformation from the 'national game' to the 'professional game' had its earliest roots in the 1870s.

1874 PECK & SNYDER SPORTING GOODS CATALOG. This drawing depicts one of the more stylish uniforms of the day, that of the Chicago White Stockings. The white uniform is trimmed with red on the pants. It also included a red belt, a red German "C" on the chest, and red trim on the shield and cuffs. The hat is also striped in red. This uniform also sports the notorious "White Stockings." The player is holding a red ball, which was used in "twilight," making it easier for fielders to see the "gloaming." (Photo Courtesy of Transcendental Graphics.)

UNKNOWN CHICAGO TEAM. The Carte de visite (visiting card) shown here is of an unknown Chicago team of the late 1860s or early 1870s. We can assume it is from Chicago because of the moniker on the left-hand side. The company that produced it, Gentile, was also from Chicago. The style of the uniform reflects that period (checkered sox and belts). Descriptions of early uniforms written in 1870, taken from the Henry Chadwick scrapbook, suggest that this may be the Eureka or Baltic team from Chicago. The Eureka team sported red and white checked stockings. The Baltic team wore light blue-checkered stockings. (Courtesy of Transcendental Graphics.)

ATLANTIC HOME RUN GALLOP. The custom of team songs was prevalent back in the early days of baseball. This is the sheet music cover to a song about the Atlantic Club of Chicago. The Atlantic Club had a long-standing rivalry with the Excelsior teams from 1859 to 1868. Unfortunately for the Atlantics, they usually came out on the losing end of these matches. (Courtesy of Transcendental Graphic.)

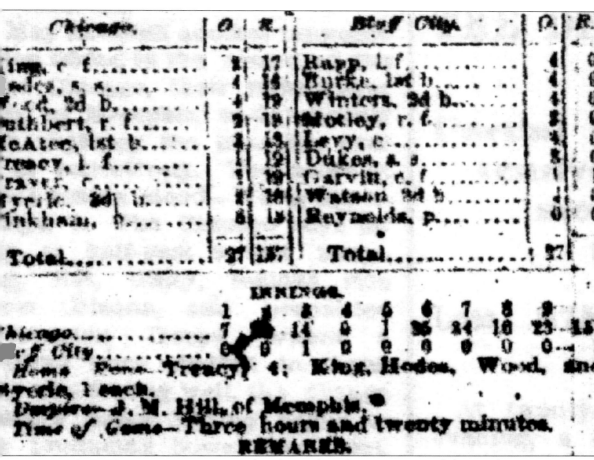

Chicago.	O.	R.	St. Jos'f City.	P.	R.
ing, c f...........	1	17	Rapp, l. f...........	4	0
sley, s. s...........	4	14	Burke, 1st b........	4	0
ek, 2d b...........	4	19	Winters, 3d b.......	4	0
thbert, r. f.........	2	19	Motley, r. f.........	8	0
cAtee, 1st b........	4	13	Levy, c.............	4	0
reacy, l. f..........	1	19	Duken, s. s.........	8	0
raver, c...........	1	19	Garvin, c. f........	1	0
rrile, 2d b.........	4	14	Watson, 2d b........	4	0
Inkham, p.........	6	13	Reynolds, p.........	0	0
Total..........	27	157	Total..........	37	1

INNINGS.

	1	2	3	4	5	6	7	8	9
Chicago.....	7	9	14	0	1	28	24	10	23—157
St. Jos'f City.....	0	0	1	0	0	0	0	0	0—1

Home Runs—Treacy, 4; King, Hodes, Wood, and
rrile, 1 each.
Umpire—J. M. Hill, of Memphis.
Time of Game—Three hours and twenty minutes.
REMARKS.

1886 WHITE STOCKING BOXSCORE. This shows the 157-1 trouncing of the Washington Olympics in September of 1886, the last year of the White Stockings championship run. It mentions in the paper that the Olympics train broke down in St. Joseph, Michigan and had to take a "day car" to the game, leaving their pitcher, Crane, exhausted. It shows in the box, where he is shown to have made fifteen errors and five wild pitches. (Research by Rational Pastimes, courtesy of the *Vintage Ballist.*)

1870 ROCKFORD FOREST CITY TEAM. Clockwise from top: Al Barker (sub., outfield), Joe Doyle (first base), Ross Barnes (short stop), Gat Stires (outfield), Tom Foley (third base), Fred Cone (outfield), Bob Addy (second base), Joe Simmons (outfield); the Middle inserts are pitcher Al Spalding (top) and catcher Scott Hastings. The 1870 Forest City team was considered professional for the 1870 season. The team was competitive, finishing with a 32-0 record against amateur teams and a 10-13-1 record against other professionals. This gives you a good idea about the diversity of teams playing in those days in the National Association of Base Ball Players. (Courtesy of Transendental Graphics.)

1870 WHITE STOCKINGS. From left to right: (front row) Levi Meyerle (third base), Ed Pinkham (pitcher), Jimmy Wood (second base), Bub McAtee (first base), and Matt King (catcher); (back row) Pearl (sub.), Ed Duffy (short stop), Fred Treacey (left field), Charley Hodes (sub.), Clipper Flynn (right field), and Ned Cuthbert (center field). The Chicago Base Ball Club got its nickname from the "White Stockings" they wore as part of their uniform. This 1870 team was the city's first attempt at professional baseball. Not since the Excelsior teams of the mid-1860s could any local club drum up enough financial support from businessmen to field a competitive nine.)(Courtesy of Transendental Graphics.)

LEVI MEYERLE. "Long Levi" was the first good hit/no field player. His coach, Jimmy Wood, said Meyerle resembled Icabod Crane and described him as tall and gangly. This fine hitter played on two occasions for the Chicago team—1870 and 1874. He was remembered more for his poor fielding—once making six errors in a game—which, due to poor field quality, was often the case in early National Association games. He was accused of helping his former team win (the Philadelphia Athletics) when the six errors were made. Meyerle also played for the Athletics in 1871, when they defeated the White Stockings for the pennant. In 1871, Meyerle hit an astonishing .492, a number that is unfathomable in any professional league these days.

1871 Chicago White Stockings. Clockwise from top: Joe Simmons (center field), Ed Pinkham (right field), Bub McAtee (first base), Matt King (catcher), E.P. Atwater (sub.), George Zettlein (pitcher), Tom Foley (third base), Charley Hodes (sub.), Ed Duffy (shortstop), and Fred Treacey (left field). Second baseman and coach Jimmy Wood is at center. The 1871 Stockings were in the hunt for the first pennant of the newly formed National Association. The National Association was formed to codify professional rules and professional teams. The White Stockings, the Philadelphia Athletics, and the Boston Red Stockings were in the hunt for the pennant until October 8th of that year. The Great Chicago Fire not only burned the city of Chicago, but also took its ball field and all the White Stocking equipment with it. The Stockings played the rest of the season on the road with borrowed uniforms and equipment. This did not hold them back from playing in the championship game against the Philadelphia Athletics. The Athletics won 4-1. Chicago would be with out a team for the next two years. (Courtesy of Transendental Graphics.)

1871 FOREST CITY.
On the outside, clockwise from the top are Osborn (sub), Ralph Ham (outfield), George Bird (outfield), Cap Anson (third base), Scott Hastings (catcher), Denny Mack (first base), Pony Sager (sub.), and Ryan (sub.) In the center are Bob Addy (second base) and Cherokee Fisher (pitcher). Not pictured are Chick Fullmer (shortstop) and Gat Stines (outfield). This was the last of the Rockford Forest City "professional" teams. Limping through the 1871 season, without the ability to attract marquee players to a small town and any real home town audience base, unlike their larger counterparts, the 1871 Forest City team finished 4-21. This did mark the first year of professional ball for a young man from Marshalltown, Iowa named Adrian Anson. "Cap," as he came to be known, led the league in doubles as a 19-year-old rookie. After the Forest City team disbanded, Anson spent the next four years playing for the Philadelphia Athletics, and then joined the Chicago White Stockings in 1876. (Courtesy of Transendental Graphics.)

1871 CHICAGO TROY. This is a wonderful picture of the 1871 White Stockings and the Troy Haymakers of Lansingburgh, New York at the Haymaker Grounds in Troy. Earlier in the year, the Chicago team refused to play the Troy nine, due to Troy's signing of Bill Craver, after Chicago suspended him. The White Stockings are the team on the left. This picture was taken two weeks after the Chicago Fire, which destroyed the White Stockings ballpark and their uniforms. As you can make out in their picture, they had to use donated uniforms from other teams. In Preston Orem's book, *Baseball 1845-1881 from Newspaper Accounts* (Self-Published 1961), Orem writes the following description: "Chicago appeared in suits of various hues and makes, ludicrous in the extreme. Pinkham wore a Mutual shirt, Mutual pants, and red stockings. Bannock, a player picked up for this eastern trip, wore a complete Mutual uniform, except for the belt, which was an Eckford. Foley was attired in a complete Eckford suit. Zettlein, 'he of the big feet,' wore a huge shirt with a mammoth 'A' on the bosom. Duffy appeared as a Fly Awayer. Some wore black hats, a few regular ball hats, others were bareheaded. Whether all this affected their play is a question, but they had not appeared so weak all season at bat. Certainly the men must have had an awfully rough time, many or most were broke, and they may have been actually hungry. Their fielding on the whole, however, was good." This picture also gives the idea of the size of the ballparks back in those days. (Courtesy of Transcendental Graphics.)

43

CHICAGO, 1871. This *Harper's Weekly* woodcut shows the city on the eve of the Great Fire that destroyed Chicago White Stocking Base Ball Park. The park can be seen to the lower,

left center of the image.

DAVY FORCE. Davy Force was a fine shortstop for his time. Force played one season for the White Stockings—1874. Though he hit .314 for the Stockings that year, it's what he did off the field that was most significant. After the 1874 season, Force signed a contract to play with the White Stockings for 1875. After signing, he also signed with the Athletic team of Philadelphia. Having signed two contracts, the National Association ruled in favor of the Athletics, citing that Chicago signed him before the season was over, infuriating the White Stockings' owner, William Hulbert. Hulbert then resolved to bring down the National Association, and by 1876 the Association was dead and the National League was formed. (Courtesy *Vintage Ballist*.)

THREE

Birth of the National League
1876–1879

In 1875, the East Coast ball teams dominated professional baseball. Teams from Boston, Philadelphia, and New York always finished near the top by attracting and keeping major stars under contract, with no option for the growing Midwest teams.

William Hulbert, raised in Chicago where he became a successful wholesale grocer, purchased the Chicago Club in 1875 and saw the East Coast monopoly as a problem. He signed the finest players in the National Association before the end of the 1875 season, which was a clear violation of Association Rules. After realizing he couldn't get away with the deed, he secretly met with owners of the "Western" clubs—St. Louis, Louisville, and Cincinnati—and they moved to form their own alliance. The league was arranged to have more control for the owners, so players could not jump from team to team as was the case for the National Association.

According to *Baseball 1846–1881*, by Preston Orem, one of Hulbert's local co-conspirators was Lewis Meacham of the *Chicago Tribune*, who in an October 1875 article had proposed a plan for a reorganization of the National Association upon the following lines:

1. All clubs must be backed by financially responsible organizations. This would eliminate the cooperatives and other weak nines, which joined the league, then failed to make road trips or to finish the season. And the Atlantics would be out.

2. No city would be admitted which had less than one hundred thousand population, an exception being made of Hartford. Thus New Haven would be eliminated as well as Keokuks and Middletowns.

3. No more than one club would be allowed from any one city. There would be no more three club deals such as Philadelphia started with in 1875. Presumably the Athletics and Philadelphia would have to consolidate.

4. The faith of the management would be shown by the deposit by each club of $1000 to $1500 before he start of the season.

The *Tribune* did not suggest the formation of a new league in the article setting forth the new plan but when Meacham, William Hulbert, who had been elected president of the Chicago club in June, 1875, and Al Spalding conferred, it practically at once became apparent that the formation of a new league was in order. For one thing one of the clubs in Philadelphia would have to be dropped and New Haven, already planning for 1876, eliminated. These changes could best be effected by simply scrapping the old and decrepit National Association.

Hulbert, in his business fashion, contacted Al Spalding of Boston and hired him to recruit the best players of the East, with the sole purpose of bringing them to Chicago for the 1876 season. And what a job Spalding did! He brought Cal McVey, Deacon White, and Ross Barnes with him from the Boston team and William Hulbert's hand-chosen player—Cap Anson, the final piece of Hulbert's puzzle—also followed suit.

Once his players were in place, Hulbert sent invitations to the Eastern teams in Hartford, New York, Boston, and Philadelphia for a meeting in New York.

Chicago, Illinois, January 23, 1876

Gentlemen:

The undersigned have been appointed by the Chicago, Cincinnati, Louisville and St. Louis clubs, a committee to confer with you on matters of interest to the game at large, with a special reference to the reformation of existing abuses, and the formation of a new association, and we are clothed with full authority in writing from the above named clubs to bind them to any arrangement we may make with you. We therefore invite your club to send a representative, clothed with like authority, to meet us at the Grand Central Hotel, in the city of New York, on Wednesday, the second day of February next at 12 M. After careful consideration of the needs of the professional clubs, the organizations we represent are of the firm belief that existing circumstances demand prompt and vigorous action by those who are the natural sponsors of the game. It is the earnest recommendation of our constituents that all past troubles and differences be ignored and forgotten, and the conference we propose shall be a calm, friendly and deliberate discussion, looking solely to the general good of the clubs who are calculated to give character and permanency to the game. We are confident that the propositions we have to submit will meet with your approval and support, and we shall be pleased to meet you at the time and place above mentioned.

Yours respectfully,

W.A. Hulbert

On February 2, 1876, the National League of Professional Baseball Clubs was formed.

The Champion 1876 White Stockings went 52-14 and won the first National League pennant by six games. The team was disassembled as quickly as it was assembled. By 1878, the team roster had changed completely with only Cap Anson remaining on the roster.

Spalding decided not to pitch after the 1876 season and was done playing with the exception of one game in 1878. In 1878, Barnes took a player-manager position with the London, Ontario Tecumsehs in the International Association. (A side note: Tecumseh Field still stands today in London, Ontario. It is now called Labatt Field. It is the oldest ballpark in North America.) White played for Boston in 1877 before meeting up with Cal McVey again in Cincinnati in 1878.

Hulbert owned the team until 1882. He won three championships in his tenure, which was cut short by a long illness and eventual heart attack at the age of 50. Hulbert not only built himself the first champions of the National League, but he also built a league that has endured 128 years and counting.

WILLIAM HULBERT. (Courtesy of Transcendental Graphics.)

ALBERT GOODWILL SPALDING.

HENRY CHADWICK.
Henry Chadwick, "The Father of Baseball," was born in England and at the age of 13 moved to Brooklyn, New York. In 1847, he began to document the game of base ball that he had grown found of. He was considered a decent short stop for secondary nines that played in wilds of Hoboken, New Jersery. Chadwick is widely known for inventing the statistics of baseball that we know today. He proposed the idea to identify the value of each ball player. At first, it was simple runs and outs; by the time he retired it had been honed to close to what it is today, featuring At Bats, Runs, Hits, and Runs Batted In. Chadwick wrote a series of ball guides from 1857 to 1888; Chadwick made the *New York Clipper* the baseball authority of its time. Chadwick continued to write about baseball up until his death in 1906 at the age of 88. (Courtesy of the *Vintage Ballist*.)

POP ANSON'S POP. Hank Anson, Cap's father, settled in Marshalltown, Iowa in the 1830s. Cap Anson was the first white child born in the town and became known as "Baby" Anson. (Courtesy of Transcendental Graphics.)

ANSON'S MARSHALLTOWN TEAM. The ball club included two Anson brothers and occasionally their father. The teenaged Baby Anson is on the top row, far right. (Courtesy of Transcendental Graphics.)

Crescent.	O.	R.	Marshall.	O.	R.
Devault, 3d base........	2	4	S. Anson, center field...	4	3
Hearty, 2d base........	3	1	Greene, catcher.........	2	5
Cavett, center field.....	3	3	Cooper, 1st base.......	3	3
Johnson, short stop.....	6	2	Coburn, right field.....	5	2
Kinsey, right field......	5	2	Parker, left field........	3	2
Dement, catcher........	5	2	A. C. Anson, 2d base...	4	2
Wells, 1st base........	3	3	H. Anson, 3d base......	3	3
Parks, left field........	2	3	Shaw, short stop.......	3	1
King, pitcher..........	4	3	Williams, pitcher.......	6	0
Total		23	Total		21

Innings	1	2	3	4	5	6	7	8	9	10	11	
Crescents	6	2	8	0	2	0	0	0	3	0	2—23	
Marshalls	6	5	2	0	5	0	0	3	0	0	0—21	

Umpire: J. B. Welch, of Occidents, Iowa Falls.

MARSHALLTOWN BOXSCORE. A boxscore featuring the Anson family, father Hank, and brothers, Ade (Cap) and Sturgis. This game was for the championship of Iowa, in either the year of 1866 or 1867. Cap at the time was 14 or 15 years old. The Marshalltown Marshalls were one of the elite teams of the state, holding the championship up until Cap's move to the Rockford Forest Citys in 1871. The Crescent team of Des Moines bested them in this championship contest for the silver ball. (Courtesy of the *Vintage Ballist*.)

YOUNG CAP. This portrait shows Anson as a 24-year old lad in 1876, his first season in Chicago. (Courtesy of David Rudd at Cycleback Press).

CAPTAIN ADRIAN ANSON. He was first known as "Baby," then "Cap," and finally "Pop." His career was the most significant in the 19th Century. He was the first member of the 3,000 hit club and nearly hit .400 when he was 42 years old. (Courtesy of Transcendental Graphics.)

CHAMPIONS. An intricate woodcut of the "1877 Champions" is actually the 1876 team. The woodcut was probably a pre-season poster to drum up support for the upcoming season. (Photo Courtesy of David Rudd at Cycleback Press.)

OUR NINE. Local pride is exhibited in this 19th century poster.

WORLD CAMPION 1876 WHITE STOCKINGS.

SCORE:

Chicago.	T	R	B	P	A	E
Barnes, 2 b.	6	3	5	4	4	2
Peters, s. s.	6	3	3	0	5	0
McVey, 1 b.	8	1	3	10	0	1
Anson, 3 b.	6	2	0	3	1	0
White, c.	6	3	1	2	0	4
Hines, c. f.	6	3	3	3	1	1
Spalding, p.	5	1	2	1	3	0
Bielaski, r. f.	5	1	0	2	0	1
Glenn, l. f.	5	1	1	2	0	1
Total	51	18	18	27	14	10
Boston.						
G. Wright, s. s	5	1	2	0	5	4
Leonard, l. f.	6	1	2	1	0	0
O'Rourke, c. f.	6	1	2	0	0	1
Murnan, 1 b	5	2	1	10	0	1
Brown, c.	4	0	1	6	3	7
Morrill, 2 b	4	1	1	7	3	0
Manning, p.	4	0	1	1	2	4
Schafer, 3 b	4	0	2	2	1	3
Josephs, r. f.	4	1	1	0	4	3
Total	42	7	13	27	18	18

RUNS SCORED.

Innings—	1	2	3	4	5	6	7	8	9	
Chicago	3	0	9	3	0	0	1	2	0	18
Boston	1	1	0	0	1	0	1	2	1	7

RUNS EARNED.

Innings—	1	2	3	4	5	6	7	8	9	
Chicago	1	0	3	0	0	0	0	0	0	4
Boston	1	0	0	0	1	0	0	0	1	3

Two-base hits—Barnes, 2; McVey, 1; Hines, 1; Spalding, 1; Wright, 1; Josephs, 1.

Three-base hits—Brown, 1.

Total bases on hits—Chicago, 23; Boston, 17.

Bases on errors—Anson, 1: White, 1; Hines, 1; Bielaski, 1—Chicago, 4. Wright, 1; Leonard, 1; Murnan, 1; Brown, 1—Boston, 4.

Left on bases—Barnes, 2; McVey, 1: White, 1; Spalding, 1; Glenn, 1—Chicago, 6. Wright, 1; Leonard, 2; Murnan, 1; Brown, 1; Morrill, 1; Manning, 1; Schafer, 1—Boston, 8.

Bases on called balls—Anson, 2; White, 1; Spalding, 1; Glenn, 1—Chicago, 5.

Passed balls—White, 3; Brown, 4.

Wild pitches—Manning, 2, Josephs, 1.

Time of game—Three hours.

Umpire—L. W. Burtis, St. Louis.

(*above*) **1876 TECUMSEH GAME**. This is a sketch of a game played in 1876 between the London, Ontario Tecumseh Club and the Chicago White Stockings. London was the champion of the International Association and the White Stockings agreed to play an exhibition. White Stocking ball player Ross Barnes, after leaving Chicago in 1877, joined the Tecumseh team in 1878 as a player manager. The interesting aspect of this print is the shape of the ball field. It is diamond shaped. This can either be attributed to the artist's conception or can it be closely related to a variation of Dr. Ford's "diamond" mentioned in the Introduction of this book. (Courtesy of the *Vintage Ballist*.)

(*Opposite page*) **1876 BOXSCORE**. This is an extraordinary look at the White Stocking lineup of the champion 1876 team. Anson hit cleanup and Al Spalding, the pitcher, hit 7th, as did his counterpart Jack Manning. This game was played in the fog. Notice under the E column, denoted for errors, the tallies on the bottom show twenty-eight errors between the two teams. This seems high, but it was the norm for the era. Remember, players did not use gloves until well into the 1880s. The *Chicago Tribune*, Wednesday, July 12th, 1876:

> *One of the extraordinary features of the game was a thick fog, which floated into the enclosure about the sixth inning, and at times covered up everything from view. Occasionally the spectators could see the fielders, and again for several minutes they could only guess at their whereabouts. This, added to the fact that the ground was covered with water to the depth of several inches in some places, made the life of an outfielder not entirely pleasant at times. It was not a good day for close fielding or scientific pitching, because the ball became after a few innings like a lump of soap, and it slid around in a scandalous manner.*

(Research by Rational Pastimes, courtesy of *Vintage Ballist*.)

CAL McVEY. Cal McVey first started playing ball at the age of 18 for the famous Cincinnati Red Stockings. Primarily a first baseman, McVey was very versatile, eventually playing every position at one time or another in his career. Though he never received many accolades from the baseball Hall of Fame, McVey's career included championships in 1869, '72, '74, '75 and '76. Five championships in 8 years with three different teams— the last with the White Stockings— is no small accomplishment. With Chicago for the 1876 and 1877 seasons, McVey batted a robust .347 and .368, respectively. (Courtesy of *Vintage Ballist*.)

DEACON WHITE. James Laurie "Deacon" White was the finest catcher of his day. A fine hitter and accurate thrower, White patrolled behind the plate for the White Stockings for only one year, 1876, but his expertise helped the White Stockings secure their first championship. Henry Chadwick was quoted as saying, "What we most admired about White was his quiet, effective way. Kicking is unknown to him. And there is one thing in which White stands preeminent, and that is the integrity of his character." (Courtesy of the *Vintage Ballist*.)

60

ROSS BARNES. Roscoe "Ross" Conkling Barnes is seen in full White Stocking regalia. The 1876 season was Barnes' last productive one. He hit .429. In 1877, the National League abolished the Fair/Four Rule. Until 1877, if a ball hit in fair territory before crossing third base, it would still be considered a fair ball. Players could purposely hit the ball down and hard and send it off into foul territory, with no play for the third or first basemen. Barnes was one of the finest at this technique, and with it disallowed his average sharply decreased. Barnes was also stricken in 1877 with an ailment "that drained was muscular strength." Some believe that this and not the Fair/Foul Rule was the reason for his drop off. (Courtesy of Transcendental Graphics.)

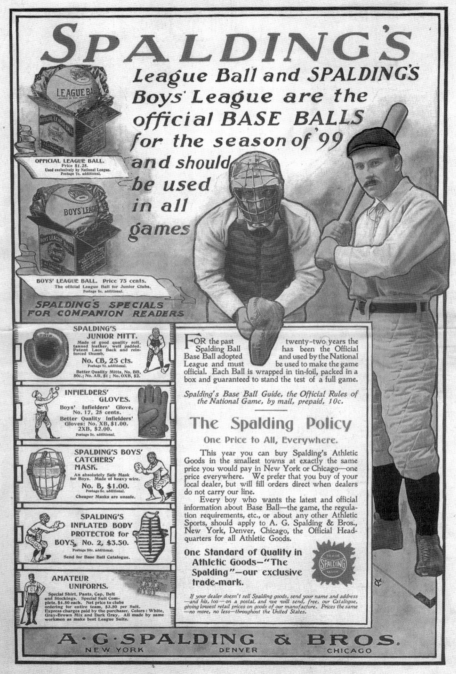

SPALDING ADS. These are three examples of advertising that was used back in the 1870s. The image on the opposite page is a Spalding Scorecard. Though out of the game by the late 1870s, Spalding kept his business mind on the game, establishing Spalding Sporting Goods, which today is still a viable member of the sporting good's industry. At right is a Cap Anson playing card, and below is an advertisement of Cap Anson shilling for an interior design company, F.C. Sheasby, in Chicago. (Courtesy of Transcendental Graphics.)

CHICAGO.

C. 1B. 4.

ANSON.

FIRST BASEMAN.

Chicago.

F. C. SHEASBY,

Wall Paper, Window Shades,

MIXED PAINTS, VARNISHES, LEADS,

OILS, GLASS, Etc.

MADISON, - - - - WIS.

OH, COME OFF!
(ANSON.)

Tobin N.Y.

BOB FERGUSON. Bob "Old Fergy" Ferguson was the player-coach for the 1878 White Stockings. Though he was only 33 at the time, Old Fergy was already a 12-year veteran in 1878. His roots began in the "old" days with the Enterprise team of New York in 1865. Old Fergy had an unspectacular career; but in 1878, his only season with the White Stockings, he had the best year of his long career, batting nearly 100 points higher than his career average. (Courtesy Trancendental Graphics.)

1878 WHITE STOCKINGS. This roster was patched together from defunct teams like Cincinnati. Anson starred along with player-coach Old Fergy. (Courtesy Transcendental Graphics.)

1879 WHITE STOCKINGS. Silver Flint and Cap Anson coached the 1879 White Stockings, who finished in fourth place with a respectable 46-33 record, 10 games behind the pennant winning Providence Grays. Anson took over the reigns in 1880, which began a championship run throughout the decade. (Courtesy of Transcendental Graphics.)

PAUL HINES. Paul Hines, an outfielder, played four years for the White Stockings in the 1870s. Hines batted .300 or better from 1874 to 1876 (.300, .315, and .331, respectively) before dipping to .280 in 1877. He went on to be a star for the Providence Grays in the 1880s, leading the Grays to the championship in 1884. (Courtesy of Transcendental Graphics.)

FRANK HANKINSON. Hankinson was a versatile player who played for the White Stockings in the late 1870s. He started out as an infielder but eventually made the switch to pitcher and became very effective with his strong arm. While his batting average dropped from .267 in 1878 to only .181 in 1879, Hankinson had 15 wins to 10 losses with a solid 2.50 ERA as a pitcher. (Courtesy of Transcendental Graphics.)

FOUR

Cap Anson and
the White Stockings

1880s

Captain Adrian "Cap" Anson was the first white child born in the frontier town of Marshalltown, Iowa, in 1852. During his childhood, the Indian natives called him Baby Anson. Anson's father, Hank, was a stern man with an affinity for baseball. Hank, a ball player himself, played for the first Marshalltown team along with Ade (Short for Adrian) and his brother Sturgis. Anson's other brother, Melville, died at the age of 10.

Word eventually got out on Anson's ball playing prowess and he was signed by the Forest City team of Rockford, Illinois in 1871 to help fill the void when Al Spalding and Ross Barnes left for the Boston team of the National Association. The Forest City team barely made it through the first professional season of the National Association, and the Philadelphia Athletics snapped up Cap Anson, where he played the next few years.

In 1876, Anson was sought after by William Hulbert and was signed as a third baseman to complete an All-Star infield. For the next 21 years, Cap Anson would set every early baseball record, collect 3,000 hits, drive in 2,000 runs, and hit over .300 19 times, all for the Chicago White Stockings. The White Stockings won the first National League Championship in 1876.

They were not to repeat until 1880, but for the rest of that decade, the White Stockings provided one of the best 10-year stretches in baseball history, winning five championships and posting a record of 691 wins and 395 losses over ten seasons. Cap Anson was a team leader, a coach, and a businessman. His arrogance turned many people off, but those who knew him closely felt that he was a just and trustworthy individual. He fought many a battle with umpires and was known to clown with the fans.

It is also believed in that Anson was the main reason that blacks were not allowed to play in the National League through the 19th Century.

His prejudice was not limited to just blacks. He wasn't very found of the Irish, either. He felt that his Irish players were nothing but a bunch of irresponsible drunks. He placed heavy fines on his Irish players for drinking and staying out late. Hugh Duffy and Malachi Kittredge seemed to have taken the brunt of his ire. In later years, he also disliked outfielder Jimmy Ryan. Anson felt Ryan "stabbed him in the bank" when he fled for the Player's League in 1890. Ryan was back the next year and the two never saw eye to eye after that. It is thought that Ryan had a lot to do with the eventual dismissal of Anson after the 1897 season. Ryan had believed that Anson's way was holding the team back. Ryan also thought the he would be next in line for the managers position. That position was bestowed on Tommy Burns, Anson's right hand man. Anson had always had a soft spot for Burns and Bill Hutchinson, for they were the only players not to jump ship in 1890.

The White Stockings were never the same after the Player's League defections. Anson held a lot of animosity against those who had left not only the White Stockings, but players from within the league. This limited Anson's ability to sign top of the line ball players.

The most amazing feat of Anson's career was in 1894. At the age of 42, Anson flirted with .400, after being talked out of retirement by the White Stockings management. Anson played 83 games that season and finished with a stellar .388 batting average.

Anson was pushed out of the organization after the 1897 season and became a successful businessman in Chicago. Anson was an orator and entertainer as well. After his playing career was over, he preformed by reading stories in theatres, and he also published a book called *A Ball Player's Career*. In the early 1900s, when baseball was at it's zenith in Chicago, Anson started what is believed to be the first baseball academy in Chicago, teaching the young and old alike the skills of the ancient game.

Another interesting development of this decade was the development of a new league and a new team for Chicago, the Browns, of the 1884 Union Association. The Union Association lasted one year and left a legacy of one team, the St. Louis Maroons, to the National League. Wealthy St. Louis businessman Henry Lucas was crazy about baseball and wanted a team in the National League. In the fall of 1883, he joined Pittsburgh promoter James Jackson to form a league to compete with the NL. They were able to attract thirty National League players with handsome salaries for the 1884 season. Lucas' team, the St. Louis Maroons, which he owned and managed, was stacked with talent and ran away with the league with a 94-19 record. The Chicago Browns weren't as lucky; they didn't finish the season. After losing the amount of $5000, the league transferred the franchise on August 25th to Pittsburgh; they became the Stogies. The Stogies must have been the dime store nickel variety, because they folded 18 games later on September 18th. The franchise was transferred to St. Paul, MN for the remainder of the league's only season. Lucas eventually got his wish and received a National League franchise in 1885 for his St. Louis Maroons.

Towards the end of the decade, Al Spalding thought it might be goodwill to send his White Stockings on a world tour playing against a team of American Baseball all stars that would accompany them on the trip. The following passage comes from a description of their farewell party from the book *Athletic Sports in America, England and Australia*, by Harry Clay Palmer, a reporter for several newspapers on the trip:

> On the evening of October 20th, a few days after the close of the season of 1888, two magnificently equipped railway coaches stood in the Union depot at Chicago, their sides ornamented by long banners of white linen upon which had been inscribed the words, "Spalding's Australian Baseball Tour." No other cars had ever stood in the great station similarly decorated, and yet no inquiries were made by the hundreds who crowded the platforms, for every well-informed traveler knew that the Chicago and All-American ball teams had played their farewell game upon the Chicago grounds that afternoon and were about to take their departure for Australia. Hundreds of baseball enthusiasts, including scores of the personal friends and admirers of the departing players, crowded the station, and it was not until a few minutes before leaving time that the members of the party bade a final farewell to the crowd, and, together with their more intimate friends and relatives, passed through the gateways and sought the neighborhood of their train, where they said their last farewells to mothers, wives, and sisters.

THE CHAMPION 1880 CHICAGO WHITE STOCKINGS. This was the first true baseball dynasty. The Chicago White Stockings, who were the first National League champs in 1876, went on to win 5 championships in the 1880s, winning the first three-peat in 1880, 1881, 1882 and then again in 1885 and 1886. Cap Anson led the White Stockings. He coached the team and was the biggest star of the game. The additions of King Kelly, Ned Williamson, George Gore and Silver Flint helped the White Stockings sustain their dominance for a full decade. (Courtesy of Transcendental Graphics.)

THE SCORE:	A	R	B	T	P	A	E
Chicago.							
Dalrymple, l. f.	5	1	3	1	2	0	0
Gore, 1 b. and c. f.	3	2	3	3	2	2	2
Kelly, c. and p.	4	1	1	2	4	2	0
Anson, 3 b., 1 b., and 2 b.	4	1	2	3	4	2	0
Burns, s. s., p., and c	4	0	0	0	3	4	0
Corcoran, p. and s. s.	4	1	3	5	0	8	0
Beals, r. f.	4	0	1	1	2	0	0
Goldsmith, c. f., p., and 1 b.	4	1	1	1	2	0	1
Quest, 2 b. and 3 b.	4	3	2	2	3	0	3
Total.	36	10	14	18	21	8	7
Buffalo.							
Crowley, r. f.	5	3	4	5	1	2	1
Richardson, 3 b.	4	2	1	2	1	3	0
Rowe, c.	5	3	2	4	1	0	0
Hornung, 1 b.	5	2	1	1	8	0	1
Moynahan, s. s.	5	3	2	3	3	0	0
Force, 2 b.	5	2	3	3	2	5	0
Galvin, p. and c. f.	5	2	3	6	2	1	0
Stearns, l. f.	5	1	3	6	1	0	0
Weidman, c. f. and p.	5	1	0	0	2	0	0
Total.	44	19	18	30	21	10	2

Innings—	1	2	3	4	5	6	7	
Chicago.	3	2	2	2	0	1	0	—10
Buffalo.	8	1	4	4	0	2	0	—19

Earned runs—Chicago, 4; Buffalo, 10.
Two-base hits—Crowley, Richardson, Moynahan, Force, Galvin, Stearns, Kelly, Anson, Corcoran (2).
Three-base hits—Rowe, Galvin, Stearns.
First base on balls—Richardson (3), Rowe, Crowley, Gore.
First base on errors—Buffalo, 8; Chicago, 1.
Left on bases—Buffalo, 8; Chicago, 5.
Struck out—Stearns, Richardson.
Balls called—Galvin, 45; Weidman, 18; Corcoran, 14; Goldsmith, 30; Burns, 41; Kelly, 38.
Strikes called—Galvin, 8; Weidman, 6; Corcoran, 5; Goldsmith, 4; Burns, 9; Kelly, 10.
Double plays—Force-Moynahan, Crowley-Moynahan.
Passed balls—Rowe, 2; Burns, 1.
Wild pitches—Galvin, 1; Kelly, 2.
Time—2:25.
Umpire—Bradley.

1880 BOXSCORE. A peek at the Champion 1880 team. Notice how the players are interchanged between positions. This was the tendency of Cap Anson's management style. Anson constantly switched players like Tommy Burns and Ned Williamson (not in this game) between third and short, depending on how well they had been fielding recently. Notice the decline in errors compared to the box score of 1876, from 28 errors to 9 in the game. (Research by Rational Pastimes, courtesy of the *Vintage Ballist*.)

WORLD CHAMPION CHICAGO WHITE STOCKINGS. From left to right: (front row) Nichol and Corcoran; (middle row) Quest, Burns, Anson, Dalrymple, and Gore; (back row) Williamson, Kelly, Flint, and Goldsmith. (Courtesy of the *Vintage Ballist.*)

E. N. Williamson, 3d B.　　　　M. J. Kelly, S. S.　　　　Frank S. Flint, C.　　　　F. E. Goldsmith, P.

J. L. Quest, S.　　　　Thos. Burns, 2d B.　　　A. C. Anson, Capt., 1st B.　　　A. Dalrymple, L. F.　　　Geo. F. Gore, C. F.

Hugh Nicol, R. F.　　　　L. Corcoran, P.

THE CHICAGO BASE-BALL CLUB.—FROM A PHOTOGRAPH BY THE PHOTO-MECHANICAL PRINTING COMPANY.—[SEE PAGE 646.]

THE CHAMPION 1882 WHITE STOCKINGS. This team was among the first to feature two star pitchers as starters. Fred Goldsmith (28-17) and Larry Corcoran (27-12) split the duties. The Chicago team won the pennant by three games over the Providence Grays. Cap Anson contributed a .362 average and 83 RBIs in 82 games played. King Kelly was also hot, hitting .305 with 37 doubles. Kelly showed his defensive versatility by playing seven different positions during the season. (Photo Courtesy of Transcendental Graphics.)

LAKEFRONT PARK IN 1882. This was the home to the White Stockings from 1878 to 1884. Located at Randolph and Michigan, Lakefront's cozy dimensions—196 to Left Field, 210 to right—

made for some interesting years of baseball in the park. (Courtesy of Transcendental Graphics.)

FRANK "SILVER" SYLVESTER FLINT. Flint, known as "Silver" for his light blond hair, was a prime example of the old time hard-nosed ball player. He began playing in the days when no gloves or masks were available and continued to field barehanded. Throughout his career, it is reported that during his tenure, he broke every bone in both hands and in his face. The New York Clipper reported, "He has few equals and no superiors as a hardworking and effective catcher, facing pluckily the swiftest and wildest pitching, being an accurate thrower to all bases." (Courtesy of Transcendental Graphics.)

	A.	R.	B.	T.	P.	A.	E.
Chicago—							
Dalrymple, l. f...	4	2	1	3	2	0	0
Sunday, c. f. & r.f.	4	0	1	1	1	0	1
Kelly, r. f. and c.f.	4	1	1	2	1	0	0
Anson, 1b.......	4	0	1	1	12	0	1
Pfeffer, 2b.......	4	0	0	0	2	6	1
Williamson, 3b..	4	2	1	3	0	1	0
Burns, s. s......	4	2	2	2	1	7	1
Clarkson, p......	4	1	1	1	0	0	3
Flint, c..........	4	0	1	1	8	0	2
Total..........	36	8	9	14	2.	24	9
Buffalo—							
Richardson, 2b...	5	0	1	1	3	4	3
Brouthers, 1b....	5	0	1	1	9	1	1
Rowe, c..........	5	0	1	1	7	2	4
White, 3b........	4	1	2	2	1	1	0
Stearns, s. s.	4	1	1	1	1	2	2
Myers, c. f.......	3	0	0	0	1	0	2
Crowley, l. f.....	3	1	0	0	1	1	0
Lillie, r. f........	4	1	1	1	1	0	0
Conway, p.......	3	0	1	2	0	10	3
Total	36	4	8	9	24	21	15

Innings—	1	2	3	4	5	6	7	8	9	
Chicago................	0	0	3	2	0	0	1	2	*—	8
Buffalo................	0	0	0	0	1	0	1	2	0—	4

Earned runs—Chicago, 3; Buffalo, 1. Two-base hits—Kelly, Conway. Three-base hits—Dalrymple, Williamson. Passed balls—Flint, 1; Rowe, 1. Wild pitch—Conway, 1. Bases on balls—Chicago, 1; Buffalo, 3. On errors—Chicago, 3; Buffalo, 2. Struck out—By Clarkson, 7; by Conway, 6. Double plays—Burns-Pfeffer-Anson. Left on bases—Chicago, 5; Buffalo, 8. Time—Two hours. Umpire—Gaffney.

In today's game on the home grounds Wood and Myers will form the battery for the visitors and McCormick and Flint for the home team.

1885 BOXSCORE.

1886 WORLD CHAMPIONS. The last championship team of the Chicago Dynasty, the 1886 club went 90-34 behind the hitting of Kelly (.388 batting average) and Anson (.371) and the pitching of Clarkson (36-17), McCormick (31-11), and Flynn (23-6). (Courtesy of Transcendental Graphics.)

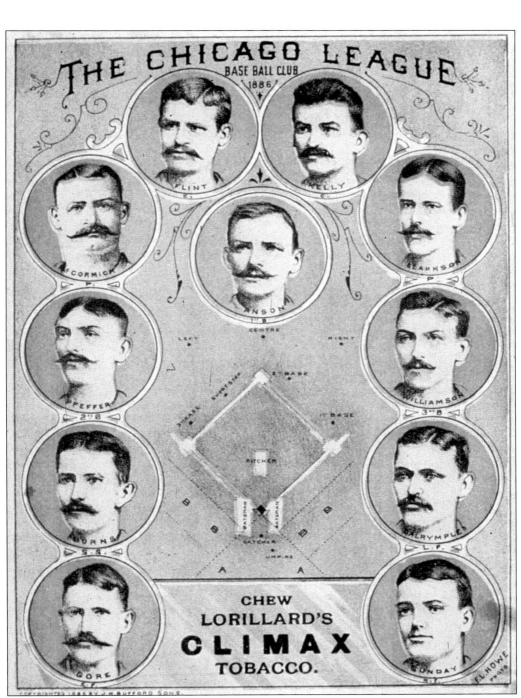

1886 WORLD CHAMPIONS. This poster shows each players' position on the field during the baseball games.

MIKE KELLY.
ALLEN & GINTER'S
Cigarettes.
RICHMOND. VIRGINIA.

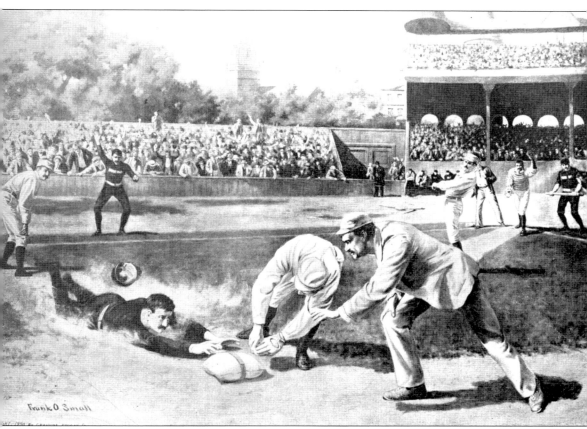

(*above*) **KING KELLY.** 1886 was the last year of King Kelly in Chicago and the championship left town with him. The White Stockings would have a few good seasons in the next 20 years, but they were not the same after Kelly left town. In 1886, King Kelly hit .388, scored 155 runs in 124 games, stole 53 bases and played all eight fielding positions over the course of the year. King Kelly was a multi talented player known for stealing third base from first base while the umpire wasn't looking. He'd also cut across the field to score from second to home, missing third base by a large margin to save time. Kelly was sold to Boston after 1886 for $10,000. He then became known as "$10,000 Kelly". He was out of all baseball a couple of years after he left the White Stockings, eventually heading to the National Association, coaching and playing for the Cincinnati Kellys. (Picture Courtesy of Transcendental Graphics.)

(*opposite*) **THE $10,000 KELLY.** Michael Joseph "King" Kelly was 22 years old when he first played with the White Stockings in 1880, and he stayed with the team until 1886. The versatile Kelly helped lead Chicago to five championships in the seven years he played with the club. Kelly was known for his off field hijinx as well as his prowess as a ballplayer. A heavy drinker, Kelly toured the stage reciting "Casey at the Bat." The nattily dressed Kelly was driven to the park in his own carriage. Kelly also wanted to be paid for use of his image. When the White Stockings traded him to Boston in 1887, for $10,000, Kelly pocketed half of that deal. On the field, Kelly would sneak across the diamond and take extra bases behind the umpires back. Once, on a pop foul, he announced himself into a game, in which he wasn't playing, and caught the ball. Many rule changes of the day were to counteract Kelly's disregard for rules. Kelly died shortly after his career was over, contracting an illness while in Boston, at 36 years of age. King Kelly was voted into the Hall of Fame in 1945. (Courtesy of the *Vintage Ballist*.)

(*left*) GEORGE GORE. George Gore was a speedy center fielder for the White Stockings from 1879 to 1886. In 1886, he drew 102 walks and had an astronomical on base percentage of .434. He was among the leaders in hits and runs scored, hitting over .300 for all but two years while in Chicago. (Courtesy of Transcendental Graphics.)

(*opposite*) 1880s VIEW OF LAKEFRONT PARK. As you can see in the center of the picture, the field is located where the modern "Streeterville" area is, the direction of where the Chicago River and Lake Michigan meet. Just below the park are the Illinois Central Railroad tracks that still exist today. Because of the cozy dimensions, 196 to left and 210 to right, in the years that the White Stockings used the park the "Ground Rule" double was introduced when the ball was hit on a fly into the stands. For one year, 1884, they decided to change it into a home run. (Courtesy of Transcendental Graphics.)

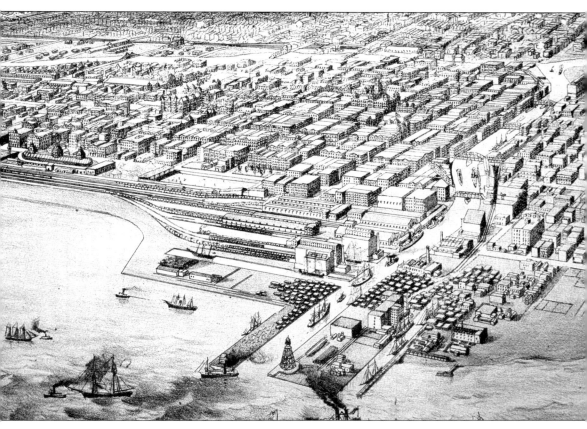

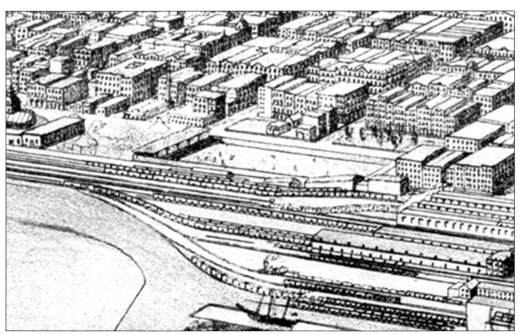

Copyright 1887
Goodwin & Co.

Clarkson, P.

WHITE STOCKINGS' ACE. Hall of Fame pitcher John Clarkson is featured on an 1888 Old Judge Cigarette Trading Card. Clarkson won 53 games for the 1885 champions (53-16) and 36 for the 1886 championship team (36-17). Clarkson played 4 more years for the Stockings before moving out to Boston. He finished his career in Cleveland, eventually losing his top pitcher status to a young pitcher named Cy Young. (Courtesy of Transcendental Graphics.)

Chicago.	R	B	P	A	E		Washington.	R	B	P	A	E
ore, c. f. ...	1	0	2	0	0		Hines, c. f...	1	1	4	0	
elly, c. & ss	1	1	5	1	1		Carroll, l. f...	0	0	2	0	
nson, 1b. ...	2	1	10	1	0		Farrell, 2b...	1	2	2	4	
effer, 2b...	4	2	3	6	0		Houck, s. s.	0	1	0	1	
'an, n, ss&c	2	2	2	3	2		Knowles, 3b.	0	1	3	1	
rus, 3b. ...	1	1	0	1	1		Crane, p...	0	0	1	2	
'Cormick, p	0	0	0	4	1		Hayes, c...	0	1	2	3	
yan, l. f...	2	1	4	0	0		Oldfield, l.f..	0	0	3	1	
ynn, r. f...	2	3	1	0	0		Baker, 1b....	0	1	7	0	
Totals ...	15	11	27	16	5		Totals...	2	7	24	12	

Innings—			1	2	3	4	5	6	7	8	9	
Chicago...			5	4	3	0	1	0	4	*—1	
Washington...			2	0	0	0	0	0	0	0—	

Runs earned—Chicago, 6; Washington, 2. Hom ns—Ryan, Farrell. Three-base hit—Anson. Two se hits—Williamson; Pfeffer, Farrell. Total base Chicago, 18; Washington, 11. Bases stolen—Flynn ines. First base on errors—Washington, 3. G lled balls—Gore (4), Kelly (4) Anson (2), Pfeffer (3 illiamson (2), Knowles. Left on bases—Chicago, 7 ashington, 6. Passed balls—Hayes, 3. Wild pitche Crane, 5. Struck out—By McCormick, 5; by Crane Double plays—Pfeffer-Anson. Time of game— urs. Umpire—Quest.

1886 BOXSCORE. This shows the trouncing of the Washington Olympics in September of 1886, the last year of the White Stockings championship run. It mentions in the paper that the Olympics train broke down in St. Joseph, MI and had to take a "day car" to the game, leaving their pitcher, Crane, exhausted. It shows in the box, where he is shown to have made fifteen errors and five wild pitches. (Courtesy *Vintage Ballist*.)

85

DELL DARLING
Champion Base Ball Catcher.

1888 Kimball Cigarette Card of Dell Darling. Darling was a back up catcher for his entire career. He played on the White Stockings from 1887 to 1889, having his best season in 1887 when he batted .319 in 38 games. It is as odd that a second tier player would have his own card in a day when such cards were scarce. (Courtesy of Transcendental Graphics.)

ANSON,
(1st Base, CHICAGO.

CHICAGO

OLD JUDGE & GYPSY QUEEN CIGARETTES

1888 Anson Playing Card.

PLAYER-TURNED-PREACHER. Billy Sunday was reserve outfielder for the White Stockings from 1883 to 1887. His modest career was overshadowed by the fact he became a world renowned Evangelist. Sunday grew up at the Glenwood (IL) Home for Boys before being moved to Ames, Iowa. He was scouted by Cap Anson and was considered the fastest player of the day. In 1887, he got "tanked up" on State and Madison and saw a gospel service. He decided to change his ways. Though he refused to play on Sunday, he played another 3 years before retiring to pursue full time Christian work. (Courtesy of Transcendental Graphics.)

Copyright 1888
Goodwin & Co.,
N.Y.

E.W. WILLIAMSON, S·S· CHICAGO.

19TH CENTURY HOME RUN KING. Ned Williamson was a powerful hitter and steady infielder, playing both short and third. Williamson smashed the home run record in 1884 with 27 when the National League ruled that balls hit out of Lakefront Park were home runs instead of ground rule doubles. His home run record would stand until a youngster named Babe Ruth broke it some 40 years later. Ironically, Williamson broke his leg in the 1888 World Tour and was never the same after that. Williamson played every season with the White Stockings with the exception of his last season, 1890. That season he played with the upstart Chicago Pirates. (Courtesy of Transcendental Graphics.)

ALL-AROUND BALL PLAYER. George (Rip) Van Haltren played a short time with Chicago from 1887 to 1889 before having great success with the New York Giants in the 1890s and early 1900s. Primarily a pitcher for the White Stockings, he became a consistent .300 hitter, playing outfield for the rest of his years. (Courtesy of Transcendental Graphics.)

OFF THE BAT. This contemporary poster mimics the action of Chicago's West Side Park.

SECOND-BASEMAN PFEFFER. Fred Pfeffer was the second baseman for the White Stockings from 1883 to 1891 and again in 1896. Pfeffer, who never wore a glove, was ranked amongst the league's leading fielders. An average hitter, Pfeffer hit 25 home runs in 1884, behind teammate Ned Williamson. Pfeffer hit 16 homers a few years later at the large West Side Grounds. (Courtesy of Transcendental Graphics.)

1888 WHITE STOCKINGS. The White Stockings finished the '88 season 9 games out of first place. Anson led the league in hitting (.344) for the last time. Jimmy Ryan led the circuit with 16 home runs. The team also went on a tour led by goodwill ambassador Al Spalding. The 53 game tour started in November of 1888 and ended in March of 1889. The team played 53 games on four continents—Europe, Asia, Africa, and Australia. (Courtesy of Transcendental Graphics.)

POPULAR 1888 GAME CARDS.

93

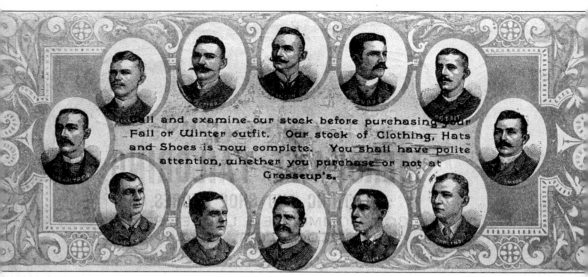

...all and examine our stock before purchasing your Fall or Winter outfit. Our stock of Clothing, Hats and Shoes is now complete. You shall have polite attention, whether you purchase or not at Grosseup's.

ADVERTISING CURRENCY FEATURING THE 1888 TOURISTS. (Courtesy of Cycleback Press.)

THE 1888 WORLD TOURISTS. Al Spalding is in the center of the poster.

TOURISTS' FAREWELL. Cap Anson shaking hands before leaving on the train west. The entourage played at Denver and San Francisco before getting on a ship for the Sandwich Islands (Hawaii). After Hawaii, they traveled to Samoa and then onto New Zealand and Australia. (Photo courtesy of Transcendental Graphics).

THE TOURISTS IN CAIRO, EGYPT.

THE TOURISTS AT THE GREAT PYRAMID.

THE TOURISTS IN ROME.

THE TOURISTS POSE OFF-FIELD.

THE TOURISTS AND FANS.

ADRIAN C. ANSON.
ALLEN & GINTER'S
Cigarettes
RICHMOND. VIRGINIA.

CAP ANSON, ALLEN & GINTER CARD, 1888. Allen & Ginter cards were the first sporting card series, using athletes from baseball and boxing, actors and other famous individuals from the era. (Courtesy of Transcendental Graphics.)

FIVE

End of a Dynasty

1890s

In 1890, John Montgomery Ward, a ballplayer with an Ivy League degree, became tired of a player's inability to play where he chose. "The Reserve Clause" tied players of that day to a team owner, and Ward sought to break it. He petitioned each and every ballplayer with the promise of independence and a players' run league. His idea was met with a warm reception and players dumped their current teams and began to sign with the rogue league.

The Chicago White Stockings, coming off a dynastic run in the 1880s, were hit hard. Only Cap Anson, mostly due to his ownership interest in the team, Tommy Burns and Bill Hutchinson, remained loyal to the team. Most of the other players jumped to the Players' League and formed the Chicago Pirates.

The Players' League only lasted one year, but the devastation to the White Stockings' team was irreversible. After making a run in 1892, the White Stockings fell to the second division for most of the decade. The only highlight being a 42-year-old Anson flirting with a .400 mark in 1894. He finished the season with a .382 average.

Anson, now called Pop Anson, was getting on in years. He was fired by the then Chicago Colts in 1897 and relieved of his coaching duties. Long time Stocking player Tommy Burns took over the helm in 1898 and finished 85-65 for a respectable 4th place. The White Stockings were then called the Orphans in reference to the team losing their "Pop".

The *Chicago Tribune* printed the following story the day it was expected that Anson would be released from his duties:

> Adrian Constantine Anson is no longer at the head of the Colts. With the expiration of his contract last night, Anson's connection with the Chicago club ceased. He has not said a word, but has waited for the club to act, while they waited for him to move. As a result the contract between the club and the veteran died an easy death, and both parties are at liberty to move their own ways. Neither has yet announced his path for the future, although both will probably have something to sat today. "I'm glad it's over," said President Hart yesterday. "We have nothing to say as yet, but perhaps the worry will cease now."

Anson merely says he will have something to say when the time comes.

A review of Anson's history is to fell only what most of the baseball world knows. In his lifetime he has taken part in more than 3000 games of ball. Think of the physical strain! Nobody has kept any accurate account, but since he began to play ball down in Marshalltown, IA, before the close of the sixties, he has faced pitchers more than 15,000 times, and probably has made3 as many as 7000 base hits. How many runs he has batted across the plate, how many times he himself has stepped upon the rubber, and how many cheers his unfailing bat has brought down only the recording angel can guess.

When Anson was discovered he, with two brothers and his father, were playing on the team at Marshalltown when the famous Forest City team of Rockford played at Marshalltown. Anson, then a big, strapping farmer boy, played second, and attracted the attention of the professionals by his cleverness. After that he attended school at Notre Dame, Indiana, a few terms. From that on his history begins to get more definite-to emerge from the mythological period, as it were. He went to the team at Freeport, IL, and after a short time changed and in 1871 played third and caught for the Forest City team at Rockford, the successors of the first great team. Anson joined the Athletics of Philadelphia, who fought Boston out for the coveted pennant. After that his record becomes more accurate, although the guides and scorers of these old days kept scant accounts of his doings. In 1874 Anson went with the Athletics on their tour of Europe, and while there achieved fame as a cricket batsman. He remained in Philadelphia until 1876. Then he came to Chicago. In those days the team with the money got the players. Anson, loyal to his first love, refused to come to Chicago, but under the persuasion of Spalding he finally forsook. Philadelphia. Since then, surrounded by a company of grand players and backed by the influence and money of Spalding, to which he has added a dignified and courageous presence, he has made for himself a fame that is worldwide. He has played in Chicago ever since. The next year after his coming the Chicagos won the pennant away from Boston and stepped to the front rank of baseball clubs in America.

Anson was always a timely hitter. Many a day will pass before a man will come whose appearance at the bat, with men on bases and a hit needed to win, will bring cheers like the coming of Anson. The greater the need the more certain was Anson to hit. Nobody can guess how many games one long drive off his bat settled. Even during his latter years, the public looked upon him as a ninth-inning savior, and the opposing twirler trembled with fear when he came up in a tight place. He could hit, and his hitting will be missed even as his kindly heart will be.

As the century ended, a new league formed out of the Western Association. Ben Johnson, a reporter from Cincinnati, was called upon as the commissioner of the league in 1894. By the end of the 1890s, Johnson felt that the Western League needed more. In 1900, he took advantage of the National Leagues downsizing and added teams in Cleveland and Chicago. Teams were quickly stocked with National League players that were victimized by the retraction. The new American League sported teams from Buffalo, Chicago, Cleveland, Detroit, Indianapolis, Kansas City, Milwaukee and Minneapolis.

In 1900, the American League was still known as a "minor" league, before standing on equal footing with the National League in 1901. Chicago's entry took an old familiar name—the White Stocking—and put a new spin on it calling themselves the Chicago White Sox early in the 1900s. A familiar man to the city, Charles Comiskey, managed the White Stockings. The White Stockings went on to be one of the most dominant teams of the early part of the 20th Century.

CHARLES COMISKEY.

WESTSIDE GROUNDS. The corner of Congress and Loomis—this was the home to the White Stockings, Colts, Orphans, and eventually Cubs. (Hint: They're all the same club, different nicknames). Also known as Congress Street Park or Westside Park, this venue was home to Chicago National League teams up until the use of Wrigley Field. (Courtesy of *Vintage Ballist*.)

1900 AMERICAN LEAGUE CHAMPIONS. Cartoon in the 1900 *Chicago Tribune* depicting Charles Comiskey hoisting the flag, much to the chagrin of Cubs President James Hart. Hart had been under fire since forcing the retirement of Cap Anson in January of 1898. (Courtesy of Rational Pastimes.)

BILL DAHLEN AND FRANK ISBELL. "Bad Bill" Dahlen played shortstop for Cap Anson and the Colts from 1891 to 1898, before being traded for his argumentative nature. Dahlen replaced Anson as team captain in 1898, but soon fell out of favor. He hit a career best .362 in 1894.

Baseball by Electric Light.

Decatur, Ill., Sept. 12.—[Special.]—Decatur a Bloomington played baseball tonight by elect light with a large crowd in attendance. The sc was 7 to 4 in favor of Bloomington.

THE "COLTS," 1890. The White Stockings had become a new team in 1890 after losing most of its team to the upstart Players League. Only Anson, Tommy Burns, and Bill Hutchinson remained from the 1889 team. The Colts, so named because of the young ages of the players, faired better than their Players League counterparts, the Chicago Pirates. The White Stockings finished in 2nd place with an 84-53 record, six games behind the Brooklyn Bridegrooms. (Photo Courtesy: Transcendental Graphics.)

(*opposite*) NIGHT GAMES. Blurb in the Chicago Tribune mentions a game of baseball being played under electric lights between the Bloomington and Decatur clubs. The interesting thing is this predates the first game played under lights by the Major Leagues by some thirty plus years. (Research by Rational Pastimes, courtesy of the *Vintage Ballist*.)

1890 PIRATES. In the early days of baseball, the media, not official names, spawned teams "nicknames." During the 1890s, the White Stockings team was so named because of their uniform's white socks. The Colts nickname was penned because of the youth of the team and, subsequently, the Orphans were named after Anson was forced out in 1897—making orphans of the players, without their "Pop." They remained the Orphans until 1901, when the American League White Sox first appeared. The name Cubs was penned by the media and also featured a young team in the early 1900. (Courtesy of Transcendental Graphics.)

BILL HUTCHINSON. "Hutch," a former star pitcher at Yale, became an ace pitcher for the Colts in the early 1890s. After breaking in as a 30-year-old rookie in 1889, Hutchinson won 42 games in 1890, 44 in 1891, and 37 in 1892. Anson personally signed him after several failed attempts to pry Hutchinson away from his Iowa farm. (Courtesy of Transcendental Graphics.)

ADRIAN ANSON. At right is the official 1892 national score card featuring Anson. Below is the cover of Anson's autobiography *A Ball Player's Career*. (Courtesy of Transcendental Graphics.)

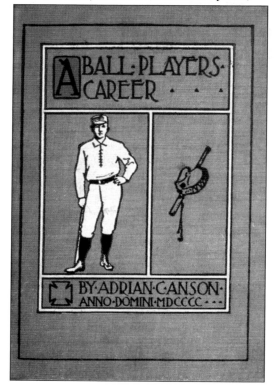

ANSON ACTION. A rare action photo of Anson playing first base. It appears to be at the old West Side Grounds. (Courtesy of Transcendental Graphics.)

ANSON ERROR. Anson is muffing a ball (making an error) in what appears to be the same game as the previous picture. Notice the dark ball. Sometimes red balls were used on cloudy days so the outfielder could see it better. (Courtesy of Transcendental Graphics.)

112

Reiley   Friend   Griffith   Parker   Ryan   McBride   Flynn
Truby   Briggs   Decker   Lange   Anson   Donahue   Everett   Terry   McFarland
Dahlen   Kittridge

CHICAGO BASE BALL CLUB, 1896.

CHICAGO BASEBALL CLUB, 1896. The 1896 Colts finished 71-57, in fifth place. This team featured Clark Griffith (23-11) who would go on to become one of the most powerful owners in the American League, of the Washington Senators. (Courtesy of Transcendental Graphics.)

ANSON AND BURNS. Tommy Burns was considered Anson's right hand man. Burns was the only position player not to jump to the Players League. Anson respected Burns for that. A shortstop/third baseman, Burns had a fairly ordinary career but was picked to replace Anson in 1898, leading the team to a fourth place finish with a respectable 85-65 record. (Courtesy of Transcendental Graphics.)

copyright 1888
GOODWIN & Co., N.Y.

RYAN JOINS CHICAGO IN 1900. Jimmy Ryan's long career started in 1885 with the championship team of 1885 and 1886. Besides a defection in 1890 to the Pirates of the Players League, Ryan finished his National League career with Chicago in 1900. Ryan wasn't very well liked. Anson thought Ryan conspired with team president James Hart to oust Anson. Ryan also beat up a sportswriter. He played for a Rogers' Park semipro team after his retirement in 1904. (Courtesy of Transcendental Graphics.)

CHICAGO UNIONS, CHICAGO'S FIRST PROFESSIONAL BLACK TEAM. Pictured in 1889 are owner and manager W.S. Peters (top, left), Captain Harry Hydes (top, right), Outfielder David Wyatt (bottom, left), and catcher Robert Jackson (bottom, right). The Unions pre-date the more-oft touring Leland Giants of Chicago by ten years. In 1890, the Unions played the first real East vs. West Championship against Cuban X-Giants of New York. In series of 14 games played in and around Chicago, the X-Giants took 9 out of 14 games, due to their superior hitting. The Page Fence Giants of Adrian, Michigan, moved their team to Chicago that same year, playing under the name Columbia Giants. Once they heard of the series, they challenged the winner of the Unions/X-Giants game. The Columbia Giants played the Unions for the city championship, the Giants winning five games to none, in front of enormous crowds. The Giants then turned their focus on the Cuban X-Giants. The New Yorkers played an 11 game series against Columbia and took 7 against 4 from the Chicago champs. (Photos Courtesy of the *Vintage Ballist*)

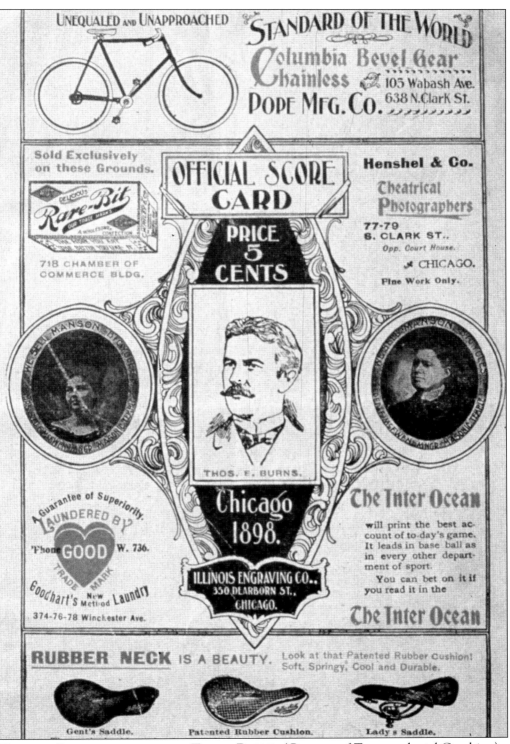

CHICAGO SCORECARD FEATURING TOMMY BURNS. (Courtesy of Transcendental Graphics.)

Kilroy
McCormick
Mertes

Griffith
Dahlen
Ryan
Lange

Woods
Isbell
Callahan
Donohue

Connor
Everett
Chance

CHICAGO BASE BALL CLUB, 1898.

1898 ORPHANS. The Orphans—so named because of the fact they lost their Pop. "Pop" Anson was asked to resign his coaching and ownership positions. He retired and opened a baseball academy in Chicago. Tommy Burns led the team to an 85-65 record, 26 games better than Anson's Colts in 1897. (Courtesy of Transcendental Graphics.)

"Pop" Anson as an old man. Anson hit .388 in 1894, when the pitching mounds were pushed back to where they are today. Several players hit over .400 that year. Why was Anson's number so special? He accomplished it at the age of 42. He was the game's first true star, carrying Chicago and the National League on his broad shoulders for the first 20 years of professional baseball. A lesser man could not have compiled what Anson accomplished. (Courtesy of Transcendental Graphics.)

"DUMMY" HOY. In 1900, the American League was still considered a "minor" league. The American League was an outgrowth of the old Western Association. In 1900, the Chicago White Stockings were a league best 82-53, 4 games better than the Milwaukee Brewers. The most notable player on this team was Dummy Hoy, a deaf and dumb mute, because of meningitis, therefore garnering the cruel nickname of "Dummy." Hoy was 5'4" and was described as "the smallest outfielder ever" by players of his day. Hoy lived to be 99 years of age. He threw out the first pitch of the third game of the 1961 World Series. He died shortly thereafter. (Courtesy of Transcendental Graphics.)

How to Read 19th Century Boxscores

1859–1869

Positions:

P	pitcher
C	catcher
1st b	first base
2nd b	second base
Sf	short field (shortstop)
3rd b	third base
Lf	left field
Cf	center field
Rf	right field

Offensive Stats:

H	Hits
HL	Hand Lost (Out)
R	Runs
O	Outs
POS	Fielding position
GP	Games played
A	Average
O Following an A	Left over or remainder (Early stats were kept as game averages, if a number was indivisible the "O" would be the number left over. This was used to determine a player's value, how many runs and outs that they would average per game.)
TB	Total Bases

Defensive Stats:

B'nd	Bound out (caught on one bounce)
Base	Put out at any base
Fly	Caught on a fly

1870–1900

Batting:

AB	At Bat
R	Runs
H	Hits
BI/RBI	Runs batted in
HR	Home Run
BA/AVG	Batting average
2B	Double
3B	Triple

Pitching:

W	Wins
L	Losses
PCT	Winning Percentage
H	Hits allowed
G/GP	Games played
IP	Innings pitched
SO	Strike outs
ERA	Earned run average

APPENDIX B

Earliest Known Illinois Teams

TEAM	YEAR	REFERENCE
Joliet Hunkidoris	1851	August 1851 *Lockport Telegraph* (via Federal Writers Project, *Baseball in Old Chicago*, 1939.)
Lockport Sleepers	1851	// //
Union	1856–67	N/A *Chicago Daily Journal* (via Federal Writers Project, *Baseball in Old Chicago*, 1939.)
Niagara	1858–60	June 1, 1858 *New York Clipper*
Excelsior	1858–68	August 1858 (via Federal Writers Project, *Baseball in Old Chicago*, 1939.)
Downers Grove	1858	July 1, 1858 *New York Clipper*
Atlantic	1858	July 18, 1859 *Chicago Tribune*
Columbia	1859	July 26, 1859 *Chicago Tribune*
Atlantic Junior	1860–68	June 9,1860 *Chicago Tribune*
Osceola	1860	October 2, 1860 *New York Clipper*
Ossawatamie	1860	// //
Bloomington	1866	June 26,1866 *Wilkes Spirit of the Times*
Freeport Shaffer	1866	// //
Freeport Empire	1866	// //
Rockford Forest City	1866	// //
Pecatonica	1866	// //
Amateur	1866–68	August 11, 1866 *Wilkes Spirit of the Times*
Eastman College	1866	// //
Mystic	1866	August 29, 1866 *Wilkes Spirit of the Times*
Belvidere	1866	// //
Garden City	1867–68	July 13, 1867 *Wilkes Spirit of the Times*
Aetna	1867–68	July 27, 1867 *Chicago Tribune*
Erie	1867–68	// //
Meteor	1867–68	July 1867 *Chicago Tribune*
Dover	1867	// //
Mutual	1867–68	// //
Eureka	1868	May 1868 *Chicago Tribune*
Northwestern College	1868	// //
Resolutes	1868	// //
Enterprise	1868	// //
Oriental	1868	// //
Liberty	1868	June 1868 *Chicago Tribune*
Dexter	1868	// //
Invincible	1868	// //
Fulton	1868	// //
Golden Rule	1868	// //
Diamond	1868	August 1868 *Chicago Tribune*
Star of the West BBC	1868	// //
Crescent	1868	// //
Mohawk	1868	// //
Evanston Monitors	1868	// //
McVickers	1868	// //

Chicago's 19th Century Champions Players' Stats

1876 WHITE STOCKINGS

BATTING:

Player, POS.	GP	AB	R	H	2B	3B	HR	RBI	AVG
Ross Barnes 2B	66	322	126	138	21	14	1	59	.429
Cap Anson 3B	66	309	63	110	9	7	2	59	.356
John Peters SS	66	316	70	111	14	2	1	47	.351
Cal McVey 1B	63	308	62	107	15	0	1	53	.347
Deacon White C	66	303	66	104	18	1	1	60	.343
Paul Hines OF	64	305	62	101	21	3	2	59	.331
Al Spalding P	66	292	54	91	14	2	0	44	.312
Fred Andrus OF	8	36	6	11	3	0	0	2	.306
John Glenn OF	66	276	55	84	9	2	0	32	.304
Bob Addy OF	32	142	36	40	4	1	0	16	.282
Oscar Bielaski OF	32	139	24	29	3	0	0	10	.209
Season Totals		*2,748*	*624*	*926*	*131*	*32*	*8*	*441*	*.337*

PITCHING:

Player	GP	W	L	W%	IP	HA	BB	SO	ERA
Al Spalding	61	47	12	.797	528.2	542	26	39	1.75
Cal McVey	11	5	2	.714	59.1	57	2	9	1.52
Deacon White	1	0	0	.000	1	2	0	3	0.00
Ross Barnes	1	0	0	.000	1.1	7	0	0	20.30
John Peters	1	0	0	.000	1	0	1	0	0.00
Season Totals		*52*	*14*	*.788*	*592*	*608*	*29*	*51*	*1.76*

1880 WHITE STOCKINGS

Player, POS	GP	AB	R	H	2B	3B	HR	RBI	AVG
George Gore OF	77	322	70	116	23	2	2	47	.360
Cap Anson 1B	86	356	54	120	24	1	1	74	.337
Abner Dalrymple OF	86	382	91	126	25	12	0	36	.330
OF Tom Burns SS	85	333	47	103	17	3	0	43	.309
King Kelly OF	84	344	72	100	17	9	1	60	.291
Fred Goldsmith P	35	142	24	37	4	2	0	15	.261
Ned Williamson 3B	75	311	65	78	20	2	0	26	.251
Charlie Guth P	1	4	0	1	0	0	0	0	.250
Joe Quest 2B	82	300	37	71	12	1	0	27	.237
Larry Corcoran P	72	286	41	66	11	1	0	33	.231
Tom Poorman OF	7	25	3	5	1	2	0	0	.200
Silver Flint C	74	284	30	46	10	4	0	32	.162
Tommy Beals OF	13	46	4	7	0	0	0	3	.152
Season Totals		*3,135*	*538*	*876*	*164*	*39*	*4*	*378*	*.279*

PITCHING:

Name	GP	W	L	W%	IP	HA	BB	SO	ERA
Larry Corcoran	63	43	14	.754	536.1	404	99	268	1.95
Fred Goldsmith	26	21	3	.875	210.1	189	18	90	1.75
Tom Poorman	2	2	0	1.000	15.0	12	0	8	2.40
Charlie Guth	1	1	0	1.000	9.0	12	1	7	5.00
King Kelly	1	0	0	.000	3.0	3	1	1	0.00
Tom Burns	1	0	0	.000	1.1	2	2	1	0.00
Season Totals	67	17		.798	775	622	129	367	1.93

1881 WHITE STOCKINGS

BATTING:

Player, POS	GP	AB	R	H	2B	3B	HR	RBI	AVG
Cap Anson 1B	84	343	67	137	21	7	1	82	.399
Abner Dalrymple OF	82	362	72	117	22	4	1	37	.323
King Kelly OF	82	353	84	114	27	3	2	55	.323
Silver Flint C	80	306	46	95	18	0	1	34	.310
George Gore OF	73	309	86	92	18	9	1	44	.298
Tom Burns SS	84	342	41	95	20	3	4	42	.278
Ned Williamson 3B	82	343	56	92	12	6	1	48	.268
Andy Piercy 3B	2	8	1	2	0	0	0	1	.250
Joe Quest 2B	78	293	35	72	6	0	1	26	.246
Fred Goldsmith P	42	158	24	38	3	4	0	16	.241
Larry Corcoran P 47	189	25	42	8	0	0	0	9	.222
Hugh Nicol OF	26	108	13	22	2	0	0	7	.204
Season Totals	3,114	550	918	157	162	36	12	224	.295

PITCHING:

Player	GP	W	L	W%	IP	HA	BB	SO	ERA
Larry Corcoran	45	31	14	.689	396.2	380	78	150	2.31
Fred Goldsmith	39	24	13	.649	330.0	328	44	76	2.59
Ned Williamson	3	1	1	.500	18.0	14	0	2	2.00
Season Totals	56	28		.667	745	722	122	228	2.43

1882 WHITE STOCKINGS

BATTING:

Player, POS	GP	AB	R	H	2B	3B	HR	RBI	AVG
Milt Scott 1B	1	5	1	2	0	0	0	0	.400
Cap Anson 1B	82	348	69	126	29	8	1	83	.362
George Gore OF	84	367	99	117	15	7	3	51	.319
King Kelly SS	84	377	81	115	37	4	1	55	.305
Abner Dalrymple OF	84	397	96	117	25	11	1	36	.295
Ned Williamson 3B	83	348	66	98	27	4	3	60	.282
Silver Flint C	81	331	48	83	18	8	4	44	.251
Tom Burns 2B	84	355	55	88	23	6	0	48	.248
Fred Goldsmith P	45	183	23	42	11	1	0	19	.230
Larry Corcoran P	40	169	23	35	10	2	1	24	.207
Joe Quest 2B	42	159	24	32	5	2	0	15	.201
Hugh Nicol OF	47	186	19	37	9	1	1	16	.199
Season Totals		3,225	604	892	209	54	15	451	.277

PITCHING:

Player	GP	W	L	W%	IP	HA	BB	SO	ERA
Larry Corcoran	39	27	12	.692	355.2	281	63	170	1.95
Fred Goldsmith	45	28	17	.622	405.0	377	38	109	2.42
Ned Williamson	1	0	0	.000	3.0	9	1	0	6.00
Season Totals		55	29	.655	764	667	102	279	2.22

1885 WHITE STOCKINGS

BATTING:

Player, POS	GP	AB	R	H	2B	3B	HR	RBI	AVG
Jimmy Ryan SS	3	13	2	6	1	0	0	2	.462
George Gore OF	109	441	115	138	21	13	5	57	.313
Cap Anson 1B	112	464	100	144	35	7	7	108	.310
King Kelly OF	107	438	124	126	24	7	9	75	.288
Abner Dalrymple OF	113	492	109	135	27	12	11	61	.274
Larry Corcoran P	7	22	6	6	1	0	0	4	.273
Tom Burns SS	111	445	82	121	23	9	7	71	.272
Billy Sunday OF	46	172	36	44	3	3	2	20	.256
Wash Williams OF	1	4	0	1	0	0	0	0	.250
Fred Pfeffer 2B	112	469	90	113	12	7	5	73	.241
Ned Williamson 3B	113	407	87	97	16	5	3	65	.238
Jim McCormick P	25	103	13	23	1	4	0	16	.223
John Clarkson P	72	283	34	61	11	5	4	32	.216
Silver Flint C	68	249	27	52	8	2	1	17	.209
Sy Sutcliffe C	11	43	5	8	1	1	0	4	.186
Jim McCauley C	3	6	1	1	0	0	0	0	.167
Ted Kennedy P 9	36	3	3	0	0	0	1	10	.083
Ed Gastfield C	1	3	0	0	0	0	0	0	.000
Bill Krieg OF	1	3	0	0	0	0	0	0	.000
Season Totals		4,093	834	1,079	184	75	54	606	.264

PITCHING:

Player	GP	W	L	PCT	IP	HA	BB	SO	ERA
John Clarkson	70	53	16	.768	623.0	497	97	308	1.85
Jim McCormick	24	20	4	.833	215.0	187	40	88	2.43
Ted Kennedy	9	7	2	.778	78.2	91	28	36	3.43
Larry Corcoran	7	5	2	.714	59.1	63	24	10	3.64
Fred Pfeffer	5	2	1	.667	31.2	26	8	13	2.56
Ned Williamson	2	0	0	.000	6.0	2	0	3	0.00
Wash Williams	1	0	0	.000	2.0	2	5	0	13.50
Season Totals		87	25	.777	1,016	868	202	458	2.23

1886 WHITE STOCKINGS

Player, POS	GP	AB	R	H	2B	3B	HR	RBI	AVG
King Kelly OF	118	451	155	175	32	11	4	79	.388
Cap Anson 1B	125	504	117	187	35	11	10	147	.37
Jimmy Ryan OF	84	327	58	100	17	6	4	53	.306
George Gore OF	118	444	150	135	20	12	6	63	.304
Tom Burns 3B	112	445	64	123	18	10	3	65	.276

Player, POS	GP	AB	R	H	2B	3B	HR	RBI	AVG
Fred Pfeffer 2B	118	474	88	125	17	8	7	95	.264
Billy Sunday OF	28	103	16	25	2	2	0	26	.243
Jim McCormick P	42	174	17	41	9	2	2	21	.236
John Clarkson P	55	210	21	49	9	1	3	23	.233
Abner Dalrymple OF	82	331	62	77	7	12	3	26	.233
Ned Williamson SS	121	430	69	93	17	8	6	58	.216
Silver Flint C	54	173	30	35	6	2	1	13	.202
Jocko Flynn P	57	205	40	41	6	2	4	19	.200
Lou Hardie C	16	51	4	9	0	0	0	3	.176
George Moolic C	16	56	9	8	3	0	0	2	.143
Season Totals		4,378	900	1,223	198	87	53	673	.279

PITCHING:

Player	GP	W	L	W%	IP	HA	BB	SO	ERA
John Clarkson	55	36	17	.679	466.2	419	86	313	2.41
Jocko Flynn	32	23	6	.793	257.0	207	63	146	2.24
Jim McCormick	42	31	11	.738	347.2	341	100	172	2.82
Jimmy Ryan	5	0	0	.000	23.1	19	13	15	4.63
Ned Williamson	2	0	0	.000	3.0	2	0	1	0.00
Season Totals		90	34	.726	1,098	988	262	647	2.54

Bibliography

Benson, Michael. *Ballparks of North America*. Jefferson, NC: McFarland, 1989

Church, Seymour. *Base Ball 1902*. Pyne Press, 1974 (reprint)

Federal Writers Project. *Baseball in Old Chicago*. McClurg Press, 1939

Morris, Peter. *Baseball Fever—Early Baseball in Michigan*. The University of Michigan Press, 2003

Orem, Preston. *Baseball (1845–1881) From the Newspaper Accounts*. Self Published, 1961

Peverelly, Charles. *American Pastimes*. Self Published, 1866

Peck, J.M. *A Gazette of Illinois*. First Published 1837, Reprint Heritage Books, 1993

Rosenberg, Howard. *Cap Anson I*. Tile Books, 2003

Rucker, Mark, *Base Ball Cartes*. Self Published, 1988

Rudd, David. *The Illustrated History of Baseball Cards Volume I: the 1800s*. Cycleback Press, 1999

Ryczek, William. *Blackguards & Red Stockings*. Jefferson,NC: McFarland, 1992

Ryczek, William. *When Johnny Came Sliding Home*. Jefferson, NC: McFarland, 1998

Seymour, Harold. *Baseball: The Early Years*. New York: Oxford Press, 1960

Society for American Baseball Research. eds. Robert Tiemann and Mark Rucker, *Nineteenth Century Stars*. SABR, 1989

White, Solomon. *Sol White's Official Baseball Guide 1907*. Camden House, 1984 (reprint)

Wright, Marshall. *Nineteenth Century Baseball*. Jefferson, NC: McFarland, 1996

Wright, Marshall. *The National Association of Baseball Players, 1857–1870*. Jefferson, NC: McFarland, 2000

GUIDES

Beadle's Dime Baseball Player	1860–1864, 1867–1871
DeWitt's Baseball Guide	1876

NEWSPAPERS

Chicago Tribune	1858–1900
New York Clipper	1857–1870
Porter's Spirit of the Times	1865–1866
Wilke's Spirit of the Times	1867–1869

OTHER SOURCES

Society of American Baseball Research
Albert Spalding Collections

Society of American Baseball Research
Henry Chadwick Scrapbook

The National Pastime, "19th Century Pictorial Issue," 1984 Society for American Baseball Research, John Thorn and Mark Rucker, editors

ARTICLES

Barash, Allison. "Baseball in the Civil War," *Vintage Baseball Association Newsletter, Baseball Players Chronicle,* Issue 1, No. 2. Fall of 2000, John Freyer, Publisher

WEBSITES

Vintage Ballist	www.vintageballist.com
The Rucker Archive	www.theruckerarchive.com
Vintage Baseball Association (VBBA)	www.vbba.org
Society for American Baseball Research (SABR)	www.SABR.org
Rational Pastimes	www.rationalpastimes.com
Baseball Almanac	www.baseball-almanac.com